MONEY
for Nothing

How to land the best deals on your
• insurances • loans • cards
• super • tax and more

Justine Davies

Wrightbooks

First published in 2012 by Wrightbooks
an imprint of John Wiley & Sons Australia, Ltd
42 McDougall St, Milton Qld 4064

Office also in Melbourne

© Justine Davies 2012

The moral rights of the author have been asserted.

National Library of Australia Cataloguing-in-Publication data:

Author:	Davies, Justine.
Title:	Money for nothing: how to land the best deals on your insurances, loans, cards, super, tax and more / Justine Davies.
ISBN:	9780730377627 (pbk.)
Notes:	Includes index.
Subjects:	Finance, Personal. Financial literacy.
Dewey Number:	332.024

Cover design by saso content & design pty ltd

Cover image: © istockphoto.com/imgendesign

Pages 100, 109: Charts from the Reserve Bank of Australia, Chart Pack, Household Sector, released 3 August 2011, from <www.rba.gov.au>

Pages 211–219: Reproduced by permission of The Treasury <www.treasury.gov.au>

Australian Taxation Office material © Australian Taxation Office. The ATO material included in this publication was current at the time of publishing. Readers should refer to the ATO website <www.ato.gov.au> for up-to-date ATO information

The CANSTAR material included in this publication was current at the time of publishing. Readers should refer to CANSTAR's website <www.canstar.com.au> for up-to-date information.

Disclaimer
The material in this publication is of the nature of general comment only, and does not represent professional advice. It is not intended to provide specific guidance for particular circumstances and it should not be relied on as the basis for any decision to take action or not take action on any matter which it covers. Readers should obtain professional advice where appropriate, before making any such decision. To the maximum extent permitted by law, the author and publisher disclaim all responsibility and liability to any person, arising directly or indirectly from any person taking or not taking action based on the information in this publication.

Foreword

No-one is born a financial guru. We all come into the world minus the money gene and struggle to learn financial skills as we grow up. I can recall in the not-too-distant past the odd relative or two dismissing acquaintances as either 'good with money' or not. To them it was that simple. Or was it? It seemed to me that those deemed not good with money were condemned to a life of reckless spending, completely oblivious to such sensibilities as providing for family and — heaven forbid — saving for a rainy day. However, knowledge is indeed power and no-one is above learning sound financial skills.

This is brought home to me every day in my work at CANSTAR. It constantly surprises me how much people genuinely do not know about the financial products they use. That's because financial products have morphed into highly complex creatures that demand attention or else seek revenge. This usually comes in the form of unnecessary fees, inflated interest rates or any other legal financial torture that can do serious damage to your hip pocket. Everyday financial products have now splintered to appeal to specialist groups in much the same way that milk is available in supermarkets as original full cream or numerous other versions with added or subtracted ingredients for this reason or that.

Too much choice can be mind-boggling. The flipside, however, is that financial products used correctly can give a much better result for a lot less when tailored to your individual circumstances. The key is clarity. Thinking clearly about your own situation, taking responsibility for the money in your life and following a plan to make that money work for your ultimate benefit is not pie-in-the-sky stuff. It's well within reach, as you will discover in the following pages.

Justine Davies will walk you through the tricks and traps of controlling your finances by demystifying financial products—for example, what are the differences between the 273 personal credit cards on the market—and de-cluttering your finances. Clearing out what's not useful or just taking up space in your money junkyard will get you on track in no time. It doesn't matter how little or how much money you earn either—the basic principles apply to all. What appeals to me more than anything is that getting on top of your money, rather than being bamboozled by it, can mean *tens of thousands of dollars* to you without an extra hour's work in your life.

At CANSTAR we applaud any effort to increase financial knowledge and skills, from budgeting and saving to investing and protecting money with the aim of attaining long-term financial security. We certainly understand how overwhelmed people must feel when dealing with their finances because we research and compare the gamut of banking and insurance products. The massive amount of data we collect on any given product sector is way more than most people could or would compare even if they had the time. This makes our research truly valuable, and we have thoroughly enjoyed working with Justine to help you transfer money stresses from the 'Too Hard' basket to the 'Why Didn't I Do This Before?' basket.

This book is bound to become a classic so treat it with the reverence it deserves, as I guarantee you will be consulting it for many years to come.

Andrew Spicer
CEO
CANSTAR

P.S. I have a confession to make about my opening sentence: I secretly do think Justine Davies was born a financial guru!

Contents

About the author

Justine Davies is a finance writer, blogger and author who loves educating people about money. Her philosophy is that the more you understand, the less you have to think about it.

Justine studied commerce at university in Victoria before moving to Queensland after receiving her degree. She worked in the insurance and superannuation industries before deciding to undertake further study and become a financial planner. Now, with more than a decade of experience as a financial planner, she writes a weekly 'Gen Y' finance column for the News Ltd papers and a weekly 'Money Stuff' blog for <www.news.com.au>.

Justine has written three previous books: *How to Afford a Baby* and *How to Afford a Husband*, both published by ABC Books, and *An Inconceivable Notion*, published by Finch Publishing.

She is also the money expert for *Women's Health* and *Practical Parenting* magazines, as well as a contributor for *Essential Baby*, and she can be heard on various radio stations across the country.

Justine currently lives in Brisbane with her husband and three children—all of whom she describes as 'priceless'!

About CANSTAR

Founded in 1992, CANSTAR is Australia and New Zealand's premier researcher of retail finance products. CANSTAR collect, analyse and research over 20 000 products within the banking, insurance, superannuation and investment industries, to provide assistance to consumers in finding the right product for their needs.

CANSTAR sees consumer education as a major part of their role and takes pride in providing fact-based data and ratings to Australian and New Zealand consumers and financial institutions.

Introduction

Dear Reader,

If you have picked up this book, it probably means that you are at least marginally interested in your finances and in wanting to improve them. And if, as Woody Allen says, 80 per cent of success is showing up, then you're well on the way to having your finances under control!

Whether it's a new exercise plan, a new diet, abolishing cigarettes from your life or a new career, often the act of making that decision to change is one of the hardest parts. Your finances are no different. It's far easier to just keep doing the same things that you've always done than it is to stop, take stock and make some improvements. Easier — but nowhere near as satisfying.

Getting your finances under control doesn't have to be difficult. After all, it's not rocket science; it's just money. You earn it, you spend it, you save it and you invest it. Sure, you have to work out a balance between all of those things to suit you personally. It doesn't have to be any more complicated than that, though.

Money for Nothing focuses on the spending and saving parts of this equation because if you don't have those basics under control, you can't effectively build for your future. Spending: we're going to cut it and redirect it. Not by making significant changes to your lifestyle—nobody wants to reduce their enjoyment of life—but by putting you in control of where your money goes. And saving: we're going to increase it. Again, not by changing your life but by getting you organised and informed. And I can guarantee that the majority of you will be amazed at just how much money you can save by putting yourself in charge.

Do you know how much of our money gets wasted? I don't mean spent on fun things such as holidays and recreation; I mean wasted because we haven't had time to shop around for a good deal on basic cost-of-living stuff. Things such as your car insurance and credit card—all those financial products that you have to have but don't have the time to research. For the average person, they cost us thousands of dollars per annum. Thousands. A few sneaky fees here, a penalty rate there…it all adds up, often to the equivalent of a hefty pay rise. Come on, this is **your money**. There are so many fun and exciting things you could do with that money—so don't just hand it over to companies who don't really need it. That's the money I'm going to show you how to save.

Money for Nothing isn't designed to be read cover to cover in one sitting. You can certainly do that, but then start at the beginning again and work through each week in turn. There are 12 main tasks that you need to complete. Some will be a breeze; others will be more challenging. They are all important though, so take your time and finish each task before you start the next one. View this book as your 12-week financial training plan—your money equivalent of a week-by-week personal fitness program—with me as the boot-camp person who shouts at you.

So, here's what I want you to do: set aside one evening each week where you will sit down and read that week's tasks.

It should only take 15 minutes or so. Then set aside two or three hours during the week—whether it's a couple of your lunch breaks or another evening—to complete the task. Try to make it the same time each week so that you can get into a routine (not that each task will necessarily take two or three hours, but just so that you're mentally prepared that it might).

And just like all good training plans, the best time to start is now. So, let's get on with it!

Justine Davies
September 2011

Get your stuff together

Getting your financial stuff together is what so many people fail to do! It's the most fundamental step towards financial security, but a lot of us don't put aside the time to do it. It's easy to live in denial: to simply earn money, spend it, earn some more, build up a bit of credit-card debt, stress about how to pay that off, ignore it and hope it goes away, vow to get a pay rise, tell your partner it's all their fault, work longer hours, keep spending…and then spend your life wondering why you never seem to be able to earn enough to keep on top of all your bills. Well, it's time to stop doing that and get your stuff together.

Quite unfairly, Gen Y seems to get the worst rap in the media for being spendthrift but, having spent a decade as a financial planner before becoming a full-time finance writer, I can tell you that there is a significant percentage of every generation who seem to muddle through life feeling constantly stressed because they never have quite enough money. And they're never quite sure where it goes, which is fine in that people are free to live their lives however they choose. But what many people don't fully appreciate is that the way you're feeling about your money situation can permeate almost every other aspect of your life.

It's serious stuff.

In 2007 the Australian government undertook a survey into people's attitudes and behaviours around money ('Financial Literacy: Australians Understanding Money'). Forty-eight per cent of adults—almost half of us—said they find dealing with money stressful and overwhelming. Now, if something you have to think about every day—and let's be realistic, you do have to think about money-related stuff pretty much every day—makes you feel stressed, then you can absolutely bet you'll carry that stress over into other aspects of your life.

Stress about money is consistently one of the top causes of relationship conflict. It's always up there in the top three, often along with other money-related issues such as over-long working hours and lack of time to spend with the family. As an example, a 2011 Relationships Australia report ('Relationships Indicators Survey', Relationships Australia/CUA 2011) found that financial difficulties or insecurities were nominated as a cause of relationship breakdown by 26 per cent of separated couples. And interestingly, those figures don't vary significantly across income levels. In other words, it's got very little to do with how much you earn and far more to do with how much you spend.

A 2011 relationships indicators survey conducted by Relationships Australia found that 71 per cent of people believe financial problems are most likely to push couples apart.

Now, in my professional experience, a lot of this stress arises because people just aren't sure what their financial situation is. On the plus side they might have a house and a car and some investments, and they earn an income. On the negative side though, they might have a mortgage and a car loan, a credit-card debt and a HECS debt, as well as the bills they have to pay every day. They're just not sure how those positives and negatives all mesh together. Nor do they know quite where all that money goes. They seem to earn a lot, but it's never enough to live comfortably.

So this week we're going to get rid of that confusion in three easy steps:

1   *Put together a balance sheet.* By listing your assets on one side of a page and all your liabilities on the other, a balance sheet helps to show you exactly what your current financial situation is.

2   *Familiarise yourself with budgets.* Budgets are actually very simple, but if you haven't done one before they can look quite complex.

3   *Put together your own personal budget.* This will show you exactly what your annual cash flow looks like. It's your blueprint for having control of your money and is what getting your financial stuff together is all about.

According to the most recent household expenditure survey by the Australian Bureau of Statistics (ABS), Aussies spend almost $1236 per week, on average, on goods and services. Many of these are essential, of course, but many are not and your budget will help you to highlight wastage. It's well worth doing: even cutting your household costs by 5 per cent could save you a tidy $3200 per annum.

(By the way — for readers who already have a balance sheet and written budget, I want you to go through the process again this week. Even if it tells you what you already know, it's a useful refresher for getting us started.)

Step 1: do a balance sheet

A balance sheet looks something like table 1.1 (overleaf).

As you can see, one side lists everything you own that has a monetary value and the other side lists everything you owe. Your balance sheet could be far more complex than the one in table 1.1 (or far simpler, depending on your stage of life). Either way, it gives you a very clear overall picture of your current financial situation. Appendix A is a balance sheet template for you to complete.

Do it now!

Table 1.1: example of a balance sheet

Assets		Liabilities	
House	$350 000	Mortgage	$280 000
Car	$15 000	Car loan	$8 000
Boat	$7 000	Credit cards	$6 000
Contents	$10 000	Store cards	$3 000
Shares	$12 000	HECS/HELP	$5 500
Cash	$4 500		
Other investments	$3 000		
Superannuation	$25 000		
Total	**$426 500**	**Total**	**$302 500**

Step 2: read through a budget

Everyone needs a written budget for so many reasons. I'll say that again: *Everyone. Needs. A. Written. Budget.* First, the process of physically putting the budget together is a fantastic way to truly understand where your money goes. Second, having it in writing is an important visual reminder of what (in expenditure terms) you're trying to achieve. Third, if you do your budget online or as an Excel spreadsheet, it's a fantastic way to keep tabs on your spending week by week to ensure you're on track.

So, we're going to do a budget and by the end of the process (if you complete it online) you'll hopefully have something that looks like table 1.2.

Table 1.2: example of a budget

Income	
Total income	$90 000
Outgoings	
Financial commitments	$34 200
Home	$12 900
Utilities	$4 700
Education	$12 800
Health	$4 560
Shopping	$12 160
Transport	$3 560
Entertainment	$3 240
Eating out	$1 040
Total income	**$90 000**
Total outgoings	**$89 160**
What's left	**$840**

Source: MoneySmart website, <www.moneysmart.gov.au>, 21/9/2011. Reproduced with permission of ASIC.

Before you start though, turn to appendix B for a budget template. Let's have a look through each section of the budget to make sure you understand what each one is for:

- *Income*. This one is pretty easy: it's what you earn. It can consist of more than just your weekly or fortnightly pay packet though, as income can include family benefits, income from investments and one-off amounts such as a tax refund. Occasionally, the government throws money around like confetti; occasionally your boss might have a good year and decide to pass on some of the profits (with any luck!).

- *Financial commitments*. These are basically any loan repayments (and don't forget to include the interest that you pay on your credit card!) plus a few other items that you may have committed to pay regularly.

- *Home and utilities.* These are also regular payments that are pretty much compulsory. Having said that, there is plenty of room for savings in this category and we will be looking into that in subsequent weeks.

- *Education and health.* These can cost a lot more than you think. For example, according to research from the Australian Scholarships Group, the cost of educating a baby born in 2011 in the public system will be $76435, an amount that increases to about half a million dollars for a private-school education. Childcare—even with the 50 per cent tax rebate—is expensive. And health costs? In a good year they mightn't be much, but in an unhealthy year they can be a considerable chunk of your bank balance.

- *Shopping and transport.* There are some massive costs hidden in this section of the budget. Groceries, for example, can be a *huge* part of your budget (you might get a shock at just how big). Gifts and transport costs can be surprising, too.

- *Entertainment and eating out.* Aaaah, this is the fun section! And you have to include it—otherwise, what are you spending all those hours at work for? You must, must, must enjoy yourself…within reason, of course! Reassuringly, we'll be leaving this section of the budget pretty much alone!

So, once you've had a look through the various sections of the budget, it's time for the moment of truth (that is, putting your actual spending habits into the budget). A budget is only as useful as the accuracy of the information it contains. I can't count how many times, in my years as a financial planner, I had clients present me with their beautifully set out, colour-coded and mathematically respectable budget. Unfortunately, the figures on their budget often bore no relationship whatsoever to the amount of money they actually spent in just about any area. In other words, they didn't have a budget at all — they just had a colour-coded piece of paper with some random numbers on it. A two-year-old could have created it, for all the relevance it had.

'My problem lies in reconciling my gross habits with my net income.'

Errol Flynn

Your budget is not an exercise in creative writing. It's not about what you would like to earn and spend or what you fondly imagine you earn and spend. For a budget to be useful it needs to show, in black and white, what you actually *do* earn and what you actually do spend in a given year. So, let's do it.

Step 3: do your own budget

You might find it helpful to follow a procedure such as this one when putting together your own personal budget.

What you'll need

To complete your budget you'll need the following:

- *Copies of all your bank statements for the past three months.* And I mean *all* your bank statements. Every single account. Your everyday account, your cheque account, your credit card and all other loan accounts, your savings account — everything. If you use online banking, it should be very quick and easy to print out your transaction history for the past three months.

- *A ruler, pen and calculator.*

- *A computer.* If you don't have access to a computer, you can use the budget template in appendix B of this book. Otherwise though, it's going to be a lot easier for you if you can jump online.

- *About two hours of uninterrupted time.* It might only take you half an hour, but be prepared for the possibility that putting together your budget could take you somewhere between one and two hours. So, rather than feeling rushed and pressured, nominate a day or evening during the week when you can sit quietly for a couple of hours to get yourself organised.

Log on to an online budget

We're going to use an online budget provided by the Australian Securities and Investments Commission's (ASIC) consumer website, MoneySmart. So jump online and go to <moneysmart.gov.au>, then click on 'Managing my Money' and 'Budgeting'. If you don't have access to a computer, use the budget template in appendix B. It's exactly the same.

If you are completing your budget online you'll notice that you have the option of either saving the budget as an Excel spreadsheet or entering the figures directly online. If you have Excel on your computer, please do it that way as you'll be able to input the individual figures as a formula (you know: the whole '= 50 + 45 + 100' type of thing) rather than using a calculator. That way there's less margin for error. Either way will be fine though.

Go through your statements

The idea here is to start at the top of the first page of each bank statement and go through every single transaction one by one. Each of those transactions needs to be put somewhere in your budget (as I said, Excel is the easiest way to do this; otherwise use your calculator to add the figures up manually as you go). Rule a line through each transaction once you've put it in the budget so you don't lose track of where you're up to.

Hopefully, most transactions will be fairly straightforward for you. Unless an entry is a cash withdrawal or deposit, the name of the business should be included in the transaction description. Can you remember what the transactions were for? A three-month period isn't too far for you to stretch your mind. Put any cash withdrawals that you just can't account for into the 'Entertainment' section, under 'Other'... but not before you've had a really good think about what the money was used for.

Don't be tempted to exclude some expenses because they were one-off items. Sure, your car may have broken down (which hardly ever happens), or your fridge may have stopped working, or the three months might have included a special birthday or Christmas. All these costs should be included though, because even if it's not your car or your fridge next year, it could be your washing machine or your computer. And if it's not Christmas or a birthday, it might be a wedding or a study tour. There will always be some type of 'one-off' expense that costs money.

Add any other costs

Once you've done all that, we're almost there. The next step is to have a think about whether there are any six-monthly or annual expenses (maybe your car registration or health insurance) and any six-monthly or annual income figures (such as a tax refund or annual bonus) that haven't yet been added in. If so, add them in now.

Double check everything

Finally, go through your budget and make sure each category of income and expenses is on the right 'frequency'. Most of them, for example, should say 'quarterly' (since we used three months' worth of bank statements). But car registration and insurance, for example, might be 'annually'. If you get paid exactly the same salary each fortnight, you might prefer to list this as a 'fortnightly' amount. You'll know what suits you.

Do one last check to make sure you haven't forgotten anything and then—congratulations! You now have an absolutely accurate, totally kickass budget!

How is it looking? Do you have a shortfall (meaning you spend more than you earn) or a surplus? Either way, don't panic—the main thing is that you know, which means you're now in control.

According to the 2007 Australian government report 'Financial Literacy: Australians Understanding Money', 48 per cent of adults don't budget regularly for their day-to-day finances.

As I said earlier, this book will basically ignore the 'Entertainment/Eating Out' part of your budget. That's your fun stuff and it's up to you to decide whether you need to cut back in that area or whether it's okay. Shopping is also really up to you: use your best judgement and common sense (oh okay, we might have a quick look at it in the final week). But what we're going to concentrate on for the next few weeks are all those financial products that you have: the car insurance, the credit cards, the bank accounts. By eliminating the fees, reducing the premiums, shopping around and being consumer savvy, these costs are where you really can find that extra 'money for nothing'.

Week 2

Fine-tune your car insurance

Okay, let's start this whole saving-money-on-financial-products thing with something that's fairly straight-forward and easy to do but which we *don't* tend to do because, well, quite frankly we've usually got better things happening in our lives. And also maybe a little bit because we've never been shown how, which is a shame because it's not difficult and it can potentially save you hundreds of dollars.

I'm talking about shopping around for your car insurance. A 2011 CHOICE report found that shopping around could net a young male driver a potential annual saving of $981, and an adult couple (or singles) $531, so it's something that's well worth spending an hour on. It really doesn't have to be any more time consuming than that.

It's also a type of insurance that's well worth having, with the federal Department of Infrastructure and Transport estimating the annual economic cost of road crashes in Australia to be about $18 billion.

Without the right insurance, being involved in a car accident can potentially set your finances (and lifestyle) back significantly—not something that anyone wants. So this week we are going to go through the following steps.

1   Understand the different types of car insurance.

2   Understand the different types of driver!

3   Learn what to look for in a policy.

4   Know how to reduce the cost of car insurance.

5   Find out how to shop around.

Realistically, going through each of the steps will take you a couple of hours. So—just as we did last week—find an afternoon or evening where you'll have the chance to be undisturbed for a while. And let's get on with it!

Step 1: types of car insurance

Before you can start shopping around for car insurance you need to decide what you actually want to be covered for. There are a few different types of insurance, the main ones being:

- compulsory third party (CTP)
- third-party property
- third-party fire and theft
- comprehensive.

Compulsory third party (CTP)

Compulsory Third Party (CTP) insurance is, as it suggests, a compulsory form of car insurance. You can't register your vehicle until you have CTP insurance in place!

What it covers

CTP gives you protection against claims for compensation if you injure or kill someone in a motor-vehicle accident. Exactly what it covers beyond that differs from state to state.

What it doesn't cover

CTP doesn't insure against the cost of any repairs to your car—or to anyone else's! Hitting someone's sports car (or caravan or boat) could set your financial goals back by several years if you only have CTP insurance. Have a look at table 2.1 for some statistics on road fatalities in Australia.

Table 2.1: road fatalities in Australia (2010 and 2011)

State/territory	Year to May 2010	Year to May 2011
NSW	185	145
Victoria	125	132
Queensland	93	104
South Australia	61	50
Western Australia	72	68
Tasmania	16	12
Northern Territory	14	7
ACT	14	7
Total	**580**	**525**

Source: Road Transport Authority, NSW.

Third-party property

This is the most basic form of optional insurance cover.

What it covers

It covers damage caused by your car to other people's property. It also covers your legal costs.

What it doesn't cover

Third-party property doesn't cover the cost of any repairs to your own car or of replacing your own car.

According to the Australian Transport Council, the average economic cost of a minor accident (no serious injury) is about $150 000.

Third-party fire and theft

If you're not wanting the full range of cover but do want some level of protection for your own car, third-party fire and theft insurance is the next option.

What it covers

In addition to covering damage to the property of others, this insurance also provides a degree of compensation if your car is damaged or lost due to fire or theft.

What it doesn't cover

It doesn't cover the cost of repairs to your vehicle if it is involved in a traffic accident. Table 2.2 shows some statistics on car theft in Australia.

Table 2.2: the chance of your car being stolen (January–December 2010)

Type of theft	Number of thefts	Theft per 1000 of population
Short-term thefts	38 693	1.73
Profit-motivated thefts	17 263	0.77
Total	**55 956**	**2.50**

Source: National Motor Vehicle Theft Reduction Council.

Comprehensive

This is the top level of insurance cover and it will certainly give you the greatest peace of mind — but it's also the most expensive!

What it covers

It covers everything mentioned in the first three insurance options. In addition, it covers damage to your own car if it's in an accident (whether the accident is your fault or not). Specific insurance policies will include other optional extras such as a replacement vehicle.

What it doesn't cover

Even comprehensive insurance has limitations. It generally won't cover damage caused by someone else driving your car, unless they were authorised to do so. It also won't cover damage caused if the driver (whether you or someone else) was over the legal alcohol limit or affected by drugs.

Additionally, your car has to be roadworthy and you must hold a valid licence.

According to the Department of Infrastructure and based on the most recent statistics available, there were an estimated 653853 reportable accidents in 2006, involving an estimated 1.16 million vehicles.

In summary

So what's covered under each of these options? Table 2.3 gives you a summary.

Table 2.3: types of car insurance

Type	Damage to your car	Damage to other people's property (e.g. other cars)	Damage or loss caused by theft of your car	Injuries or death to other people in an accident
Compulsory third party (CTP)	No	No	No	Yes
Third-party property	No	Yes	No	No
Third-party fire and theft	No	Yes	Yes	No
Comprehensive	Yes	Yes	Yes	No

Source: MoneySmart website, <www.moneysmart.gov.au>, 18/8/2011. Reproduced with permission of ASIC.

Step 2: types of driver

Okay, so you know what types of insurance cover are out there, and also your rough chances of needing it. But before you can start looking for a policy you need to have an understanding of what type of driver you are. You can forget the Constitution and whatever the Australian Human Rights Commission might tell you because when it comes to cars, all drivers are *not* created equal—not in the eyes of insurance companies, anyway. So it's useful to know how they are likely to view you.

What is your driver profile?

Young drivers — male/female under 25

You are likely to have a lower-value car and perhaps even one at-fault claim on your record. From a car insurance point of view, the sex of young drivers can make a difference, with young males deemed a bigger risk, according to road crash statistics.

Male/female drivers mid-to-late 20s

An accident-free driving record means that drivers aged 25 to 29 have progressed to a rating 1. By now, you may have a medium-priced car (maybe valued somewhere around or under $20 000) and hopefully no-one under 25 will be driving this car! The difference in sex, while not as crucial as in the young, first-time drivers, can still be of significance to some car insurance companies.

Drivers aged 30–59

As there are no young drivers to be considered with this profile, you can absolutely benefit from competitive prices. Hopefully you will qualify for the full no-claim bonus and with a regular cash flow will be able to save even more on annual premiums by covering minor incidents with your own money. A typical car value of around $30 000.

Executive car drivers — over 30

With more disposable income, you can afford a more expensive car. Sure, the car costs extra to insure but hopefully you would qualify for the full no-claim bonus — and there are likely to be no additional drivers to complicate matters.

Family — with at least one young driver

The stereotypical family consists of mum, dad and perhaps a son and daughter who are both aged under 25.

The family wishes to insure a car, valued at under $30 000, for the entire household to drive.

Mature drivers — over 60

These long-time drivers are looking for a hassle-free policy that provides a few more features to make their lives easier, should they have to make a claim. By now your car has probably been downsized from a family 'swagger wagon' to something more practical—maybe valued at under $20 000. Plus, you have no young drivers to complicate matters!

Low-kilometre drivers

If you fit this profile, then irrespective of your age the insurance premium is entirely dependent on the kilometres driven. This type of insurance is perfect for that second car that sits at home most of the time and does fewer than 10 000 kilometres per year.

Source: CANSTAR <www.canstar.com.au>.

Of course, a 'typical' driving profile may not suit you if you have—shall we say—an unusual driving record. Or if you have a non-standard sort of car. Or if you live somewhere that's considered to be incredibly high (or low, for that matter) risk. In those types of situations you might need a bit of extra research to find the best deal.

Step 3: decide what you want

Just as all drivers are not created equal, all insurance policies are not created equal. A 'standard' policy can differ significantly from provider to provider. At the end of the day, the more inclusions you have on your policy, the more expensive it's likely to be, so it will depend on your personal preferences (and perhaps driving habits!) as to what you include or exclude. But there are some questions to ask.

Agreed or market value?

You can either insure your car for an agreed value (that is, a specific dollar value) or market value (that is, what your car is worth on the market at the time of the accident). An agreed value will give you the peace of mind of knowing that you could afford to replace your car if you needed to; market value is likely to give you a cheaper premium.

What's an excess?

Most insurance policies have an 'excess', which is the amount you will have to contribute towards the repair before the insurance company will begin to contribute. You can generally nominate the dollar value of excess that you are willing to pay (it can range anywhere from zero to $1000 or more). An extremely low excess will result in a higher premium, but a very high excess will mean you may end up out of pocket for minor damages.

Are there discounts?

If you have an exemplary driving record, you could be eligible for a no claim bonus. If that's you, some companies will offer you a discount on your premium.

Who can be insured?

As a rule of thumb, the more people you have as authorised drivers under your insurance policy, the more expensive the cover will be—especially if any of them are under 25. It's important to weigh up the balance between cost and the practicalities of day-to-day driving life.

What's included?

Theft and accident are obvious inclusions under standard cover, but you should also ensure that you'll be covered for weather events such as hail or floods, and incidental damage such as vandalism.

What 'extras' are included?

Different policies will have different 'extras', which may include things such as a replacement hire car while yours is being fixed, roadside assistance, no excess for windscreen repairs, no excess for lost car keys, a multiple policy discount and insurance cover for personal contents within the car. Choice of repairer is something included as a standard on some policies and featured as an extra on others.

Complete table 2.4 to work out which extras you might need from a policy.

Table 2.4: what's important to me

Extras	Must have	Would be nice	Don't care
Agreed value			
Small excess			
Discount for no claims history			
Multiple drivers			
Cover for adverse weather events			
Replacement car			
'No excess' windscreen repair			
Roadside assistance			
Choice of repairer			
Cover for personal contents			

Step 4: reduce the cost

Now that you're (no longer) thoroughly confused about what you should be looking for, let's look at some of the things that might help to make your car insurance premiums a bit cheaper.

House your car safely

Having your car locked and garaged securely at night and parked safely during the day can make a difference to your premium cost.

Take a test!

Designed specifically for drivers aged under 25, some insurance companies will offer a discount on premiums if you complete a skilled-driving test. So if you're a young driver, it's worth asking the question!

Add safety features

Adding safety features such as (for older models) an immobiliser or a car alarm can also be a plus.

Keep your driving record clean

Okay, this one isn't completely within your control of course, but if you *do* have a squeaky-clean driving record, it helps!

Limit who can drive your car

I have already mentioned the 'who can drive your car' issue; obviously the fewer people who are authorised to drive your car, the cheaper your premium could be.

Limit the plastic surgery!

The turbo charger, the aerodynamic body kit, and the oversized exhaust...even the fluffy dice. The more modifications you make to your originally modest vehicle, the higher your insurance premium is likely to be. Well, in truth, the fluffy dice probably won't make a difference.

Compare quotes

As I said at the beginning of the week, a recent CHOICE report found that the average adult could save more than

$500 each year (and a youngish male could save more than $900) by shopping around.

Specifically, according to CHOICE's 2011 Car Insurance Comparison and Review report at <www.choice.com.au>, you could potentially save the following on car insurance:

- $981 for a young male driver
- $531 for an adult couple (or singles)
- $637 for an adult couple with an at-fault accident (or singles)
- $472 for an older couple (or singles).

Step 5: shop around

There are numerous providers of motor vehicle insurance, and it would be physically impractical for you to contact and compare policies from each one. To give you an idea, the 36 general insurers in Australia who are registered with the Financial Ombudsman Service at <www.fos.org.au> and provide motor vehicle insurance are:

- Comminsure <www.commbank.com.au>
- COTA <www.cota.com.au>
- Dawes Underwriting <www.dawes.com.au>
- Elders Insurance <www.insurance.elders.com.au>
- Famous Cars Insurance <www.famousinsurance. com.au>
- GIO <www.gio.com.au>
- Guild <www.guildgroup.com.au>
- HBF <www.hbf.com.au>
- Insurance Made Easy <www.madeeasy.biz>
- Jardines Lloyd Thompson <www.jlta.com.au>
- Just Car Insurance <www.justcarinsurance.com.au>

- MB Insurance Group <www.mbinsurance.com.au>
- MTA Insurance Ltd <www.mtai.com.au>
- NRMA <www.nrma.com.au>
- One Path <www.onepath.com.au>
- Progressive Direct <www.progressivedirect.com.au>
- QBE <www.qbe.com.au>
- RAA Insurance <www.raa.com.au>
- RAC <www.rac.com.au>
- RACQ <www.racq.com.au>
- RACT <www.ract.com.au>
- RACV<www. racv.com.au>
- Real Insurance <www.realinsurance.com.au>
- Ryno Insurance Services <www.rynoinsurance. com.au>
- SGIC <www.sgic.com.au>
- SGIO <www.sgio.com.au>
- Shannons <www.Shannons.com.au>
- St Andrew's Insurance <www.standrewsaus.com.au>
- Suncorp Insurance <www.suncorp.com.au>
- Swann Insurance <www.swanninsurance.com>
- Territory Insurance Office <www.tofi.com.au>
- Tokio Marine <www.tokiomarine.com.au>
- Toyota Insurance <www.toyotainsurance.com.au>
- Virginia Surety Company, Inc.
- Westpac <www.westpac.com.au>
- YOUI <www.youi.com.au>.

By the time you finished working your way through the offerings of each of those insurers, it would be time to start the process again!

So, instead:

- *Ask friends and colleagues.* Sometimes a great way to narrow down the search for a product is to find one on referral. In other words, ask friends and colleagues who they use and—importantly—if they would recommend the company, particularly in the area of claims service. While this may not seem all that important when you're comparing the price of policies, a survey by CANSTAR found that 34 per cent of respondents had made a claim in the last three years, with about 45 per cent being very satisfied with the claims service and another 30 per cent being somewhat satisfied. As your only interaction with the claims department is likely to be if something bad happens, good service can be vitally important. You might be flustered, emotional, even injured. You want good service!

- *Harness the power of modern technology.* That is, jump online and try out a comparison website or two. While comparison sites do have a limitation in that they rarely cover every single policy available in the marketplace, they will almost certainly cover a far broader range than you could possibly do by yourself. Some websites to try are: <www.canstar. com.au>, <www.ratecity.com.au>, <www.infochoice. com.au>, and <www.mozo.com.au>.

- *Contact your existing insurer.* Finally, of course, don't hesitate to contact your existing insurer to see what else they can offer. They are likely to have far more policies available than just the one you're already signed up for. Figure 2.1 (overleaf) shows people's overall claims service satisfaction. Sometimes the prospect of losing your custom can make them, well, just a bit more competitive.

Figure 2.1: overall claims satisfaction

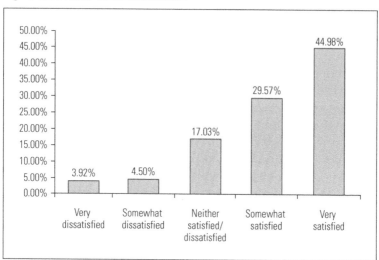

Source: CANSTAR <www.canstar.com.au>.

So that's it. A few hours of research and dedicated work and you're now an expert in car insurance! Well, at any rate you have a better understanding of what types of insurance are out there, what type of driver you are and what insurance policy conditions are important to you personally. You've also learned how to go about finding a good deal. As I said at the start of the week, shopping around for car insurance isn't exactly exciting stuff—we've usually got better things happening in our lives. But saving up to $981 per annum—not just this year, but each year that follows—is definitely worth the investment of your time. Just think what else you'll be able to do with that money!

Good luck!

Week 3

Health check your health insurance

This one is a bit more complex, but there are potentially hundreds of dollars in savings to be made by gritting your teeth and getting on with it. According to a June 2011 comparison report by the Australian Consumers Association, people with family cover could, by shopping around, save:

- $559 to $1529 per annum on top hospital cover with no excess
- up to $1320 per annum on top extras.

So let's do it.

From a low of about 30 per cent in 1997 to 45 per cent today, membership of private health funds has been steadily increasing, thanks largely to some carrots and sticks that the government has introduced. These include:

- *The Medicare levy surcharge.* In 1997 the government introduced the Medicare levy surcharge. This is an extra 1 per cent of tax levied on taxpayers who earn more than a certain amount (currently $77 000 for a single person or $154 000 for a family) if they do not have private health insurance. So let's say, for example, that your taxable income is $85 000 — the

Medicare levy surcharge will take an extra $850 for the government, thank you very much.

- *The private health insurance rebate.* At the same time as it introduced the mentioned surcharge, the government also introduced a subsidy scheme to help taxpayers with the cost of their insurance cover. After a few changes, this became the private health insurance rebate that we currently have, whereby health insurance holders are reimbursed 30 per cent of the cost of their insurance premium. So, for example, if your annual health insurance premium is $1200, you'll receive $360 of that back. You can claim this in your tax return or claim it as a reduced premium whenever you pay. While there is ongoing debate around means testing this benefit (that is, not giving it to higher income earners) it's currently available to everyone.

- *The lifetime health cover loading.* Commenced in July 2000, the lifetime health cover loading is designed to encourage you to take out private health insurance while you're young and healthy rather than leaving it until you're older and more likely to need it. After all, the health funds have to try to stay solvent! What it means in dollar terms is that if you don't have private health insurance by the first day of July following your thirty-first birthday and then decide to take out hospital cover later in life, you will pay a 2 per cent loading on top of your premium for every year you are aged over 30. So, for example, a 40-year-old taking out cover for the first time will pay 20 per cent more than a 30-year-old with the same cover.

According to the government's COAG Reform Council, the median waiting time for elective surgery in 2009–10 was 35 days, rising to 264 days for those waiting the longest. Private health insurance means skipping this queue!

Given these incentives, the bottom line is that even if you truly believe yourself to be invincible (which, let's face it, none of us really are), it can make good financial sense to have private health insurance anyway. And if you do already have it, then it makes incredibly good financial sense to shop around for it.

Why have private health insurance?

Private health insurance gives you the peace of mind of knowing that you and your family will be covered should any health problems crop up. It means you circumvent public hospital waiting lists which, for an elective operation in a public hospital, can be lengthy. In addition to this waiting period, operations are put in order of priority, meaning that you may have to wait for an operation, only to be told that it has been pushed back for another patient whose situation is more critical.

Private health members enjoy a waiting period that is substantially less and can sometimes be immediate. Those with private health insurance also have the security of a 'locked-in date', meaning that their operation will not be pushed back due to another patient's needs.

Finally, with private health insurance you can select your preferred doctor or surgeon to carry out an operation. However, in a public hospital, your doctor will be the one on duty at the time of your operation.

Source: CANSTAR <www.canstar.com.au>.

Do you know what you're actually covered for under your current policy? Chances are: no. And you're in good company, with an iSelect report last year finding that 43 per cent of private health insurance policyholders have only a rough idea of what they could potentially claim on.

That's not surprising, because private health insurance is confusing. There are thousands of different policies on the market and they all have different levels of cover, different excess amounts, different inclusions and exclusions and different waiting periods and cut-off limits and ... oh well, the list just goes on and on. It can all seem too overwhelming and that's a big reason why — as Private Health Insurance Administration Council (PHIAC) CEO, Sean Gath, admitted to me — people tend to leave it in the bottom drawer. Let's change that!

This week we'll go through the following steps:

1   Know what types of insurance cover there are.

2   Get an idea of the health-funds market.

3   Decide what's important to you.

4   Read your current policy document.

5   Put together a shortlist.

6   Make some calls and choose a fund.

Now, don't freak out about the number of steps. Some of them will take you five minutes! Others will take you slightly longer though, so set aside two or three hours.

Step 1: types of cover

This might sound obvious, but it's handy to understand that there are three types of health insurance: hospital cover, ancillary cover (extras) and packages.

Hospital cover

Hospital cover insures your treatment in hospital. (Yeah, I know: duh.) It covers some or all of your hospital costs that aren't met by Medicare. This may include things such as accommodation, theatre fees, tests, doctors' fees and so forth. Basically, having hospital cover gives you the flexibility to decide whether you want to be treated as a public patient in a public hospital, as a private patient in a public hospital or as a private patient in a private hospital. Policies will differ on exactly what hospital treatment they will cover — and even at which hospital.

Ancillary cover

This is your 'extras'. This is your insurance cover for non-hospital related things that aren't covered by Medicare—things such as dental, optical, physiotherapy, chiropractic and home treatment. It might also include treatments such as acupuncture and a gym membership contribution.

Packages

These are basically packages that combine hospital and ancillary cover in the one policy.

Step 2: study the market

Yes, there are hundreds of different policies…but they're all provided by just a handful of insurers: 39 of them, to be exact. And of that 39, 13 of them are 'restricted' (meaning they are only available to certain occupation groups). So really, there are only 26 general funds. All 39 are listed in table 3.1 (overleaf).

There. Aren't you feeling so much more positive about this whole exercise now that you know the size of the market!? Some of these funds will be familiar to you — often because they have very large marketing budgets — and others will be new. They're all worth checking out!

According to ABS data, health costs have consistently risen at a greater rate than inflation over the past seven years.

Table 3.1: health funds in Australia

Health fund	Web address	Type	Available in
ACA Health Benefits Fund	<www.acahealth.com.au>	Restricted	All states
Australian Health Management	<www.ahm.com.au>	Open	All states
Australian Unity Health Limited	<www.australianunity.com.au>	Open	All states
Bupa Australia Pty Ltd — ANZ Health Insurance	<www.bupa.com.au>	Open	All states
CBHS Health Fund Limited	<www.cbhs.com.au>	Restricted	All states
CDH Benefits Fund	<www.cdhbf.com.au>	Open	All states
Central West Health Cover	<www.centralwesthealth.com.au>	Open	All states
CUA Health Limited	<www.cuahealth.com.au>	Open	All states
Defence Health Limited	<www.defencehealth.com.au>	Restricted	All states
GMF Health	<www.gmfhealth.com.au>	Open	All states
GMHBA Limited	<www.gmhba.com.au>	Open	All states
Grand United Corporate Health	<www.guhealth.com.au>	Open	All states
HBA — Bupa Australia Pty Ltd	<www.hba.com.au>	Open	ACT, NSW, QLD, TAS, VIC, WA
HBF Health Limited	<www.hbf.com.au>	Open	All states
HCF	<www.hcf.com.au>	Open	All states
Health Care Insurance Limited	<www.hciltd.com.au>	Restricted	All states
Health Insurance Fund	<www.hif.com.au>	Open	All states
Health Partners	<www.healthpartners.com.au>	Open	All states
Latrobe Health Services	<www.latrobehealth.com.au>	Open	All states
Manchester Unity Australia Ltd	<www.manchesterunity.com.au>	Open	All states
MBF — Bupa Australia Pty Ltd	<www.mbf.com.au>	Open	All states

Health fund	Web address	Type	Available in
Medibank Private Limited	<www.medibank.com.au>	Open	All states
Mildura District Hospital Fund Ltd	(03) 50 217 099	Open	All states
Mutual Community — Bupa Australia Pty Ltd	<www.mutualcommunity.com.au>	Open	SA, NT
National Health Benefits Australia Pty Ltd	<www.onemedifund.com.au>	Open	All states
Navy Health Ltd	<www.navyhealth.com.au>	Restricted	All states
NIB Health Funds Ltd	<www.nib.com.au>	Open	All states
Peoplecare Health Insurance	<www.peoplecare.com.au>	Open	All states
Phoenix Health Fund Limited	<www.phoenixhealthfund.com.au>	Restricted	All states
Police Health	<www.policehealth.com.au>	Restricted	QLD, SA, TAS, WA, NT
Queensland Country Health Fund Ltd	<www.qldcountryhealth.com.au>	Open	QLD
Railway and Transport Health Fund Limited	<www.rthealthfund.com.au>	Restricted	All states
Reserve Bank Health Society Ltd	1800 027 299	Restricted	All states
St Lukes Health	<www.stlukes.com.au>	Open	All states
Teachers Health Fund	<www.teachershealth.com.au>	Restricted	All states
Teachers' Union Health	<www.tuh.com.au>	Restricted	All states
The Doctors' Health Fund	<www.doctorshealthfund.com.au>	Restricted	All states
Transport Health Pty Ltd	<www.transporthealth.com.au>	Restricted	All states
Westfund Ltd	<www.westfund.com.au>	Open	ACT, NSW, QLD, WA

Source: <www.privatehealth.gov.au>.

Step 3: decide what's important

There are hundreds of different health insurance contracts available; working through which ones are relevant to you is a vital step in this whole process, because the key to saving money on health insurance is only paying for stuff that you need or are likely to need. Many of the policies out there have plenty of stuff included that you just don't need.

So, how do you work through which ones are relevant to you? To a certain extent this will depend on what your personal situation is right now. See whether you recognise yourself in any of these typical lifestyle profiles.

What is your lifestyle profile?

Young single

Young to middle-aged single (male or female) with no dependants and no immediate plans for children. While you probably don't consider yourself to be invincible, you are likely to be mostly concerned about having a safety net for hospital cover if you ever need it. Dental, optical, chiropractic and physiotherapy cover are also important areas of extras cover.

Established single parent

This profile covers mostly middle-aged to mature singles with older but still dependent children (or child). These families have stopped growing so no longer need cover for obstetrics and IVF. The parent is starting to think about cover they might need for their growing kids such as orthodontics but they are also thinking about other areas of cover they might have ignored when they were younger such as cardiothoracic surgery. Dental, optical, physiotherapy and chiropractic cover are also important areas of extras cover.

Young families/couples (with obstetrics)

Young to middle-aged couples with a young child or children, as well as couples planning a family. A relevant description is 'expanding families' and while you are not yet concerned about cover for hip replacements and multi-focal lenses, you're interested in cover for obstetrics and IVF, dental, optical, physiotherapy and chiropractic. Couples planning for children in the short-term should be taking out the appropriate family cover now!

Young couples (no obstetrics)

This profile covers young to middle-aged couples who don't plan to have children or at least are postponing a family. You are probably looking for all-round cover from your health fund but don't need to pay for obstetrics and IVF. A good hospital plan with extras such as dental, optical, physiotherapy and chiropractic should provide all-round cover for you.

Young families (no obstetrics)

There will be no more kids!! Young to middle-aged couples with a young child or children, and who will not be extending the family. You are confident that you will not be needing obstetrics or IVF cover! Nevertheless, there's a distinct need for a range of hospital and extras cover for both you and your kids.

Established families

This profile covers mostly middle-aged couples with older but still dependent children. Your family has stopped growing so there's no need for obstetrics and IVF. You're probably focusing on cover for your growing kids, such as orthodontics … but you might be also thinking about areas of cover that you've previously ignored, such as cardiothoracic surgery. Dental, optical, physiotherapy and chiropractic cover are also important.

What is your lifestyle profile? *(cont'd)*

Mature singles/couples

The kids have left home! Woo-hoo! Now, we're not suggesting that age is catching up with you but you might be starting to seriously consider areas of cover such as cardiothoracic surgery, hip replacements or multifocal lenses. Due to the natural processes of ageing, your health insurance requirements differ from that of young singles. Dental, optical, chiropractic and physiotherapy are also important areas of extras cover.

Source: CANSTAR <www.canstar.com.au>.

In other words, what you should consider including in your health insurance policy will depend on your stage of life, as well as personal preference. In addition to inclusions, you can play around with excesses and coverage to match a policy and a premium that suit you. So get a pen, turn to appendix C (a health insurance checklist) and answer the following questions.

How much hospital cover do you need?

This is where your 'lifestyle profile' (in the box) comes into it. Look, emergency lifesaving treatment is going to be provided in a public hospital no matter what level of private cover you have (or whether you have it at all). That's a level of treatment that everyone is entitled to via Medicare. Beyond that though, you can choose to specifically include or exclude treatment for various conditions or negotiate payment limits on certain conditions. That's what makes the difference between a *top level* of insurance (that must cover all services where Medicare pays a benefit), a *medium level* (that may restrict the amount of benefit the insurer will pay for certain conditions) and a *basic level of cover* (that will have a number of exclusions, such as pregnancy, eye surgery, hip and knee replacements, rehabilitation and cardiac services. Think carefully before excluding conditions — you never know what might happen. But, of course, the higher your level of cover, the higher the cost.

What is your family history?

Look at your family history when thinking about what cover you need. Some conditions can be genetic: mentally noting any hereditary illnesses that close family members have had will assist you in identifying the inclusions you might want in a policy. Also, look back through your medical receipts to check what you personally have claimed on over the past year or two.

How much excess can you afford to pay?

The 'excess' is the amount of money you will have to pay before your private health insurance kicks in. The higher your excess, the cheaper your insurance premiums. An excess typically ranges from zero to $1000.

Can you afford a co-payment?

A co-payment is sometimes used as an alternative to an excess. It's generally a daily amount that you personally have to contribute if you're receiving hospital treatment. It's usually a set dollar amount per day, and the total amount you may be liable for in any one year is often capped — although it's important to note that some policies may have 'no limit'.

Can you afford a gap fee?

The 'gap' is the potential difference between what your hospital and doctors charge and the amount Medicare and your health insurance fund between them will pay. So, for example, a doctor's fee of $100 might be subsidised up to $40 from Medicare and a further $40 from your health fund, leaving you to pay the gap of $20 from your own pocket.

Some funds offer 'gap cover' so you can be assured that you won't end up out of pocket. Again, though, this will increase the premium.

Which hospitals are covered?

Insurance funds often strike agreements with particular hospitals, meaning they will cover your costs if you end up in one of those hospitals, but may not cover you (or may require you to pay significant out-of-pocket amounts) in another hospital. It's not as restrictive as it sounds — most health funds have agreements with a wide range of hospitals — but it is something you need to keep in mind. The government's private-health information website <www.privatehealth.gov.au> has an excellent search tool that you can use to determine whether a particular health fund has agreements with the hospitals in your area.

Do you need extras?

All right. So we've covered the main hospital-related considerations — now how about extras? As I said earlier, that's your dental, optical, physio and so on. Decide which extras you need.

In 2010, private-health insurers paid $1.6 billion of the $3.3 billion charged for dental services (49 per cent). Insurers pay more benefits for dental services than any other type of general treatment, amounting to almost 52 per cent of benefits paid out, followed by optical at 18 per cent. For more information on this fact, go to <www.privatehealth.gov.au>.

Step 4: read your policy document

In a moment we're going to embark on finding you the perfect fund ... but how do you know that you don't have it already? (If you have an insurance policy at all, that is.) So, dig out your policy document (or download it online) and have a quick read through it to work out what cover you already have. As you've been through the question and answer process, all that small print will likely make a bit more sense than it otherwise would.

Step 5: make a shortlist

You might be feeling a bit dubious about this step, given that there are so many insurers to choose from. Fortunately though, technology makes it, well, if not easy then at least a more straightforward process than it would otherwise be. Online comparison shopping ... we love it when it comes to buying electronic goods, shoes, fashion and makeup (admit it, you have eBay bookmarked on your desktop), but we've been a bit slower to embrace it when it comes to looking for financial products. It can certainly simplify the process though, particularly if you know what you're looking for—which you now do.

So, there are a number of websites that have online comparison tools to help you select a health fund including: Private Health Insurance Ombudsman <www. privatehealth.gov.au>, CANSTAR <www.canstar.com.au>, iSelect <www.iselect.gov.au>, Moneytime <www.moneytime. com.au>, and Help Me Choose <www.helpmechoose.com.au>.

Your first online port of call should be the government's private-health website. However, online comparison sites have different methods (different parameters) that they use to match your policy needs. So, I recommend that you also try at least one other online comparison website—just to be thorough!

Each of the websites will ask you a series of questions, which you will be able to answer easily now that you've completed appendix C. Now cross-check the list of options with the hospitals that you want to be covered for. Remember that you can do that at <www.privatehealth.gov.au>. Try to narrow your search to about five policies.

Step 6: make some calls

If you're confident that you've found the ideal health cover, you can simply apply for the insurance online right now. But if you're still unsure about anything—have any niggling questions—then pick up the phone and call the insurers on your shortlist. A few examples of questions that may still be swirling around in your head are:

- What waiting periods apply?
- Is ambulance cover included?
- What are the annual claim limits?
- Is there a discount for multiple policies?

Also, of course, don't hesitate to phone your current insurance provider to see whether they can match the features and premium of a rival policy. It's always worth asking the question.

Be aware that if you remove a particular condition from your cover and subsequently add it back on, you may have to commence your waiting periods all over again.

Once you have done that, complete the paperwork! But...make sure you don't cancel your current health insurance before the new one is in place. Your new insurer can arrange the cancellation for you or you can choose to do it yourself.

Some more tips

Here are just a few more tips on how to get the best from your chosen fund.

Make sure you claim

Yes, it might sound obvious, but sometimes it's easy to forget what your policy includes and whether it's claimable. So double check—and always claim where you can.

Have your card handy

Keep your health fund card in your wallet. It can be easy to pay the medical bill, file the paperwork away and just not get around to sending it to your health fund. One way around this is to pay via the Health Industry Claims and Payments Service (HICAPS) wherever possible. HICAPS is the method of claiming electronically at the point of service (the doctor's surgery, dentist, physio and so on). It's a much more efficient way of claiming—but usually you need to have your health fund card with you to do it.

File your receipts

Keep all your receipts in the one place for any possible tax offset. I'll cover this again in week 11, but basically, for any out-of-pocket medical expenses above $2000 during the financial year (that is, the amount you personally had to pay after any health fund or Medicare refunds were paid) you can claim a 20 per cent tax offset on the excess. However, you'll need to keep all your paperwork in one place so you can tally it up at the end of the financial year for your tax.

Pay on time

Keep your premium payments up to date! Most funds will not pay any benefits for treatment if your premiums are not up to date. And if you fall more than two months behind, the fund may cancel your policy. This would mean a whole new application and a whole new set of waiting periods!

Know your limits

Know the annual limits for your extras cover. When it comes to items such as your dental, optical and physio, funds usually impose a maximum annual benefit they will pay. It's useful to know what these maximum benefits are so you can (where possible) regulate your use. Funds also differ on what they define as 'annual'; that is, your annual benefit might be calculated on a calendar year (meaning that work done in December and work done in January would be considered as two separate years). Alternatively, they may use a financial year or may calculate it as 12 months from the date of your last treatment.

Get a record of costs

You can contact Medicare <www.medicare.gov.au> for a printout of all medical costs claimed through Medicare over the year. The statement will show the total cost of treatment, the benefit refunded, and the out-of-pocket costs.

And now, you're done! Fantastic effort! From here on in, your weekly projects are going to seem like a breeze!

Supersize your super

I know, I know, you're just not that into it. Superannuation doesn't interest you. It's *years* before you retire and you can't access your money any earlier. Plus the government keeps changing the rules—they've made more than 2000 changes to the legislation since 1992. Who knows whether the money will even *be* there in a few decades? The government will probably work out some way to get their hands on it between now and then. Even if they don't, you're:

- planning to live fast and die young
- never going to retire
- expecting the world to be destroyed by choking pollution and rising oceans before then
- intending to win lotto
- just not that into it.

Okay, so I'm being facetious, but it's amazing how many people take little or no interest in their superannuation, despite the fact that it's likely to be one of their most significant sources of money in the future. About 80 per cent of people, to be precise. I'm sure, of course, that you're in the interested minority. Either way, it's big business. According to the most recent statistics, there's currently about

$1.3 trillion in superannuation, a figure that's projected to rise to $5 trillion over the next 15 years. That's a big pot of gold at the end of the rainbow!

And we can all benefit (sometimes hugely) by putting aside a few hours to get our superannuation organised. As there are some phone calls you will need to make, arrange for at least one hour of that time to be during the day. As a quick overview, these are the steps that we're going to cover:

1   Choose the superannuation fund that suits you (because a small change in your investment return or ongoing fees can have a massive cumulative effect on your retirement nest egg).

2   Choose a specific investment that suits your risk profile. Once you've chosen your overall fund, you need to choose how you want your money invested. Shares? Property? Cash or bonds? Or a mixture of them all?

3   Find and consolidate your superannuation (because more than half of us have at least two superannuation funds. And possibly more that we don't even know about).

4   Tidy up the loose ends. Should you put your insurance through superannuation? Who should you nominate as your beneficiary? Should it be binding?

5   Question whether or not you should be paying extra. For some that will be an emphatic 'no way', but for others at a different stage of life it could make a lot of financial sense.

So, if you're ready, let's get started!

Step 1: choose a fund

Choosing a superannuation fund entails finding a product that has cost-effective fees and an overall good long-term performance outlook.

It doesn't have to be complicated—but for the sake of your future retirement it is something that you have to do and take an active interest in because, whether you like it or not, at least 9 per cent of your salary goes into your super fund. If you're an employee, superannuation is something you have to have! It's a big chunk of your future retirement income, and fund performance and fees can vary massively between investments. On an average income, a 1 per cent lower management fee, for example, can potentially make about a $50000 difference to your retirement account balance in today's dollars. An extra 2 per cent return on your money can make more than $100000 difference—again, in today's dollars. Give the superannuation calculators at <www.moneysmart.gov.au> a try—you could get a shock! In table 4.1 I've used one of them to show the difference a 1 per cent reduction in fees would make.

Table 4.1: fee reduction for a 25-year-old planning to retire at age 65

Current superannuation balance	$10000	$10000
Current annual salary	$65000	$65000
Current employer contribution	$5850 (9% of $65000)	$5850 (9% of $65000)
Administration fee	**3% per annum**	**2% per annum**
Total fees at retirement, in today's dollars	$197361	$146901

As you can see in table 4.1, simply reducing the fees by 1 per cent and keeping everything else the same will mean an extra $50000, in today's dollars, at retirement.

So, with everything else (salary, years to retirement, investment performance, contribution amounts) remaining equal, the simple act of reducing the annual fee on your superannuation fund can make tens of thousands of dollars' difference, in today's dollars, to your retirement nest egg. Table 4.2 (overleaf) shows the result a 2 per cent increase in return would make.

Table 4.2: performance boost for a 25-year-old planning to retire at age 65

Current superannuation balance	$10 000	$10 000
Current annual salary	$65 000	$65 000
Current employer contribution	$5 850 (9% of $65 000)	$5 850 (9% of $65 000)
Administration fee	2% per annum	2% per annum
Investment return	**7.5%** **(before fees and tax)**	**9.5%** **(before fees and tax)**
Account balance at retirement, in today's dollars	$285 661	$429 814

So, increasing the return by 2 per cent and keeping everything else the same will mean an extra $144 000, in today's dollars, at retirement.

All other things remaining equal, finding a fund that provides you with an extra 2 per cent return per annum over the long term could potentially boost your retirement savings significantly, with nothing extra for you to do.

Of course, the worst-case scenario is that you end up in a fund that has both high ongoing fees and a lower long-term return. Check out table 4.3.

Table 4.3: the worst of both worlds — a 25-year-old planning to retire at age 65

Current superannuation balance	$10 000
Current annual salary	$65 000
Current employer contribution	$5 850 (9% of $65 000)
Administration fee	3% per annum
Investment return	**7.50% (before fees and tax)**
Total fees as at retirement, in today's dollars	$197 361
Account balance at retirement, in today's dollars	$235 201
Total fees as a percentage of final balance	45%

In other words, if you have the bad luck to end up in a superannuation fund that has comparatively high ongoing fees *and* a comparatively lacklustre return, you could end up frittering always almost half of your nest egg in fees.

That's right: higher fees and a lower return means you could potentially be halving your retirement funds.

Of course, this won't happen to you — because you're going to take an active interest in where your money is invested, right?

(As a side note, the government is in the process of introducing some protection for workers against this high fee/low return scenario, with the development of MySuper. Part of the recent Super System Review recommendations undertaken by the government, MySuper will be designed to provide a simple and cost-effective product that will be the default account for workers who do not nominate a specific super fund. It's scheduled to all be in place by July 2013. *But*, the retirement buck stops with you. It is absolutely your responsibility to take an interest in where your nest egg is invested.)

Only 20 per cent of investors actively choose their superannuation investment option.

Before you start looking, it may be useful for you to know some history with regard to how superannuation has developed in Australia. I don't mean legislatively, but in terms of the *types* of fund on offer.

Unless you're going to go to the trouble of setting up your own self-managed super fund, there are two types of fund you can choose from: industry funds and retail funds. Here's a rundown from CANSTAR.

Industry funds versus retail super funds

Debate continues over the differences between industry and retail superannuation funds. Which is the best? That's a matter of personal opinion, but we can tell you how they differ. Industry funds and retail funds differ in their history and structure. They can be likened in some ways to credit unions and banks. Here's a brief rundown.

Industry funds versus retail super funds (*cont'd*)

Retail funds were developed by financial institutions and insurance companies to cater for people who were interested in investing and saving for their retirement. It's fair to say the initial focus of these funds was wealthier white collar customers, typically in management positions. They offered investment expertise and personal service to their clients and charged a commission to provide that service. The funds were developed to generate revenue and profit for the financial institutions.

In response, trade unions argued that a comfortable retirement should be available to all workers, not just management. Therefore industry funds were predominantly developed by trade-union and industry bodies to provide for their members in retirement. Until recently they were exclusive to their industry but super choices have opened them up to anyone eligible for superannuation. This is where the term 'public offer' originated — they are now open to the general public and no longer restricted to their industry.

Industry funds are not-for-profit organisations. When it comes to the products offered there can be considerable differences in the fees charged. Because industry funds are not-for-profit they generally charge lower fees. However, this is changing. Some retail funds are now challenging this paradigm by introducing new low-cost products — for example, AMP Flexible Super Core and Select. Retail funds tend to offer a much greater range of investment options. However, we are seeing signs of industry funds responding with new options. For example, Sunsuper now offers 20 options including single-sector and emerging-market investments. There is also the argument that too many options is not actually beneficial.

One source of historic difference has been commissions. Industry funds will tell you they don't pay any commissions to financial advisers. And let's face it the lower the fees the more money goes in your account and the better off you will be. However, as the old saying goes, there are always two sides to every argument. The other side of the argument is if you get good advice and invest in the right option you will be much better off in the long run—even if you pay fees to your financial adviser. And there are ways to minimise the fees and commissions you pay.

When it comes to advice, retail funds generally have a much stronger focus on promoting advice services and providing advice through their own adviser channels or arrangements with an adviser network. This is no surprise given their history. We surveyed 1100 superannuation account holders and asked who had obtained financial advice in the past 12 months. Overwhelmingly, retail fund customers had a higher percentage of customers who had obtained financial advice in the past 12 months by a ratio of more than 2 to 1.

This is not to say industry funds don't value advice as many have established call centres staffed with qualified advisers, or enter into arrangements with adviser groups. They can answer simple super questions right through to full financial plans.

Source: CANSTAR <www.canstar.com.au>.

So, whether it's an industry fund or a retail fund, the majority of workers are able to choose a superannuation product that suits their needs and which they are personally comfortable with (double check with your employer, just in case!). And as I said at the start, that means finding a fund with competitive fees that has had a healthy long-term return. Let's start looking!

Competitive fees

While the general rule of thumb is that retail funds traditionally have higher total fees than industry funds, choosing a low-fee fund can still be easier said than done. Some funds have so many different fees!

Retail funds traditionally have higher total fees than industry funds. As an example, a Chant West research report in 2008 found that the average fund management fee for a retail fund is 1.69%, while the average fund management fee for an industry fund is 0.83% — about half the cost.

Understanding fees

Basically, super funds charge five major fees on your superannuation.

Membership fee

Super funds charge a membership fee; that is, a fee for you to be a member with them. This is usually a weekly fee and it varies from $1 to $5 per week.

Administration fee

These are also known as management fees. This fee is charged by super funds for looking after or managing your super account; for example, issuing statements and so on. Mostly these have a tiered fee structure; that is, based on your super balance you will be charged a certain percentage on your balance. The higher your super balance, the lower the percentage of fee applies, although the total dollar cost will be more as your balance grows.

Management Expense Ratio (MER)/investment cost

MER is the fee charged by your fund manager for managing your investment. This fee is based on your choice of investment. The fee is usually charged as a percentage of your super balance.

Performance fee

This is the fee charged by fund managers for being able to exceed the target performance for the year. Most of the funds will provide an estimate for the coming year rather than the exact fee. This is because fund performance is not known until the end of the year and the performance fee is based on whether or not the fund manager outperforms the market. Some of the funds include this in their MER while others show it separately in their Product Disclosure Statement (PDS).

Contribution fee

Usually charged while making contributions to your super account, this fee is payable to your financial adviser for their recommendations. Usually this fee is negotiable with your adviser and it varies from zero to 5 per cent. This means that for every $100 paid into your account, the account may be credited with only $95.

Source: CANSTAR <www.canstar.com.au>.

Ugh, so many possible fees being deducted from your retirement money! And of course, in conjunction with that, the next thing to consider is the long-term returns.

Healthy long-term returns

Choosing a superannuation fund that has a record of good, consistent long-term performance is essential. It *can* be tricky, given that there are hundreds of different investment options out there, but fortunately the wonders of modern technology (that is, online comparison sites) can make it a bit easier. Of course, past performance is no guarantee of future performance and your goal shouldn't be to dump all your money into the super fund that has shot the lights out in the past year or two. Nevertheless, the past long-term return should hopefully be a good indicator of the quality of management and investment discipline made by the superannuation fund.

Now, when I talk about healthy long-term returns I don't just mean on one specific investment option. Sure, a superannuation fund may have had a stellar return on its commercial property fund, for example—but perhaps it really bombed on its balanced fund, or its Australian shares fund. It would be unusual for a superannuation fund to have incredible growth across its entire investment range, but what you're looking for is respectable, consistent returns over time across a broad range of investment options. (And of course, when markets are really dire, what you're looking for is a fund that has managed to contain its losses as much as possible.) But a consistent pattern of return over time is generally an indication of responsible management.

So once you're ready to research your fund options, jump online and give one of these comparison sites a try: CANSTAR <www.canstar.com.au>, Chant West <www. chantwest.com.au>, Selecting Super <www.selectingsuper. com.au>, and SuperSavvy <www.supersavvy.com.au>.

And hey—make sure you research your current fund—you could find that the one you have is already perfectly suited to you!

Step 2: choose a suitable investment

Your investment type should suit your risk profile. So what is a 'risk profile' anyway? If you've ever been to see a financial planner, you're probably familiar with the term; otherwise maybe not. Basically, your risk profile is an indicator of how comfortable you are with volatility (change in price). It measures your willingness to potentially accept short-term losses in pursuit of higher long-term gains. Your risk profile combined with your investment time frame will help a financial adviser to determine the types of investment that will best suit your needs.

Your risk profile is an indicator of how comfortable you are with volatility (change in price).

I'll elaborate: appendix D outlines the main types of asset class that you can invest your money into. These asset classes are cash, bonds, property and shares. The different asset classes traditionally have different levels of volatility. So cash, for example, has low volatility. The value of the asset doesn't change suddenly. Shares, on the other hand, go up and down every day. In other words, they are more volatile. Answering the question of how comfortable/ uncomfortable you are personally with the idea of your investments changing in value from day to day helps to determine your 'risk profile'.

Investors are usually classed as one of the following:

- *Cash only.* These investors are not at all comfortable with the idea of any volatility within their investment. They would prefer to accept a lower long-term return for the peace of mind of having no volatility.

- *Conservative.* These investors are not very comfortable with the prospect of high volatility in investments. They are willing to hold some growth investments (such as shares or property) in their portfolio but prefer the majority of their money to be in cash or fixed interest.

- *Balanced.* These investors are comfortable with the prospect of some volatility as a tradeoff for high long-term returns. They prefer a majority of growth investments but also like to hold some cash investments to smooth out the risk.

- *Growth.* These investors are very comfortable with short-term volatility as a price of long-term growth. Their portfolio would focus on shares and property.

This description, then, becomes your risk profile. When it's combined with your investment time frame, it helps guide you to the types of broad asset classes you should be considering.

Ask questions about super

When it comes to choosing the mix of investments for your superannuation savings, there are a couple of basic questions you need to ask yourself before making a decision:

- How much risk do I feel comfortable taking?
- What type of return am I seeking for my money?
- What time horizon am I investing to?

The answers to these questions will help guide you in choosing the right investment mix or option for your superannuation savings.

Source: The Association of Superannuation Funds Australia.

With regard to superannuation (and the fact that you can't get at it until you hit retirement age), your investment time frame will depend on your stage of life. The type of 'risk profile' you're likely to belong to is outlined in this MoneySmart chart in figure 4.1.

Figure 4.1: types of risk profile

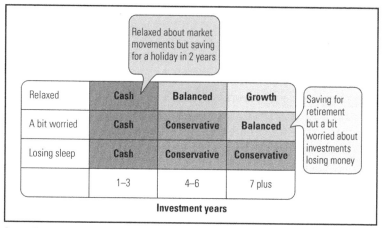

Source: MoneySmart website, <www.moneysmart.gov.au>, 21/09/2011. Reproduced with permission of ASIC.

Remember, though, that the explanation and chart is a very general overview; everyone is different. The way you personally react towards the idea of volatility could vary greatly from that of your colleague or your partner or your neighbour, even if you are all at the same stage of life. For that reason it's important to (1) trust your inner voice of caution and (2) discuss risk profiles and investment options with a licensed financial adviser.

A rule of thumb when it comes to working out how much risk you are prepared to take with your superannuation savings is the 'sleep at night' principle. Whatever the level of risk you take, it shouldn't be sufficient to keep you awake at night. If it is then you're probably out of your comfort zone.

It's also very important, as you've probably realised by reading through all this information, to be actively involved in the management of your superannuation through every life stage. Even though it's something that happens automatically and which we can't touch for aeons, superannuation is *not* just a set-and-forget thing. The investment choices that suit you at one life stage will not suit you at another. Review them regularly!

The following information is from the Association of Superannuation Funds of Australia.

New risk guidelines

In June 2012, new industry guidelines will come into effect, which will standardise the disclosure of investment risk in superannuation funds.

Under the guidelines, superannuation funds will provide a 'Standard Risk Measure' ranging across seven risk bands, from 'very low' to 'very high', for each of the investment options they offer, and will disclose the risk of negative returns over a 20-year period for each of their investment options. This will make it a lot easier for consumers to better understand the investment risk in the option they have chosen and make it easier to compare funds on a like-for-like basis.

Source: The Association of Superannuation Funds Australia.

Step 3: find your super

Nineteen billion dollars. Not million—*billion*! That's how much money is sitting in 'lost' superannuation accounts in Australia. And as almost half of all workers have at least one lost superannuation fund out there somewhere, chances are some of it could be yours. As well as the millions of lost accounts, there are also countless duplicate accounts that we may well know about but just haven't bothered consolidating. All those accounts add up to billions and billions of dollars of retirement money *and tens of millions of dollars in duplicate fees* that are achieving nothing except extra profit for the investment companies.

Some of that money could be in your pocket!

So, there are two elements to finding your super. One is to consolidate all the accounts you know about. The other is to search for any superannuation you may have lost along the way.

Consolidate your accounts

Once you have chosen your preferred fund in step 1, this is actually pretty straightforward. Phone your superannuation fund for (or download from its website) a transfer form: one for each of your duplicate accounts. Fill them out, include a certified copy of your drivers licence (most funds ask for proof of identity before they will transfer your money) and post them away. Done!

Find your lost superannuation

This one is a bit trickier, although the Australian Taxation Office (ATO) keeps a Lost Members Register, to which all of the superannuation funds have to report. You can access this via the ATO's website at <www.ato.gov.au>. Type 'SuperSeeker' into the search box. Alternatively you can telephone the SuperSeeker line on 13 28 65 and give them your name, date of birth and tax file number.

Of course, this search will only work if your tax file number has been recorded against the account, which historically wasn't always the case. After trying the SuperSeeker option, if you feel you still have outstanding money somewhere, make a written list of all your employers and give them a call, one by one. Ask them which fund your superannuation may have been paid into...and start the paper chase. Fun, fun, fun!

It can be exhausting work tracking down your super, but it can be a very worthwhile process and a welcome boost for your future retirement nest egg!

Remember that you are paying account-keeping fees on every superannuation fund that you have. Consolidating your superannuation into one fund can slash these duplicate fees and save you a lot of money!

Step 4: tidy up loose ends

You've chosen your superannuation fund and rolled all your other accounts into it. You've done all the hard work — congratulations! There are just a couple of small details to tidy up before we're finished though!

Nominate a beneficiary

Who should get your money if you die? It sounds pretty straightforward, but there are a couple of issues to be aware of when it comes to superannuation and the 'what if' scenario.

The first thing to know is that superannuation isn't part of your estate. Unlike your car and your house and any other worldly possessions you own, you cannot dispose of your superannuation through your will. That's because your superannuation isn't really yours — not yet, anyway — it's simply being held in trust for you. Once you reach retirement age you can take direct ownership of it, withdraw it all and blow it on whatever you choose. Until that point, though, the money is being held in trust for you and it is the trustee of the superannuation fund who has the final say over who gets the money if something happens to you.

That doesn't mean you shouldn't nominate a beneficiary though, because it will certainly give the trustees some guidance on who might need to be considered in the event of a payout.

However, it's important to know that trustees are restricted in who they can pay your superannuation to. Under the relevant legislation, the trustees of a superannuation fund must pay the benefits to your legal personal representative or to any or all dependants you may have. So, nominating your neighbour or favourite nephew or a charity is almost guaranteed to cause problems. And, tellingly, issues about payment of death benefits make up more than one-third of all complaints received by the Superannuation Complaints Tribunal. It's a contentious issue!

Binding death benefit nomination

Some superannuation funds give you the option of making a binding death benefit nomination. In this instance, the trustees of the superannuation fund are bound to follow your instructions with regard to payment of the benefit. A binding nomination is only valid for a period of three years though, so it needs to be updated regularly.

It's important to note that death benefits can only be paid to the estate of the member or to a dependant under the Superannuation Industry (Supervision) SIS legislation. A binding nomination made to anyone else won't be valid.

Always discuss the pros and cons of binding nominations with your superannuation fund before you make one!

Insurance within superannuation

Consider whether or not to have your insurance within superannuation: I'm talking about your personal insurance here—your life cover, total and permanent disability and your income protection. Each of these insurances can be applied for (and paid) within your superannuation fund. There are advantages and disadvantages either way.

Advantages

- *It doesn't cost you anything now.* Because the insurance premiums are paid from the money that's in your superannuation account, it's a way of having insurance without having the cost of it eating into your day-to-day budget.

- *It can be cheaper upfront.* Because superannuation funds negotiate insurance deals for thousands of people, they can access bulk discounts in premium costs. This means the cost of the insurance cover could be cheaper within superannuation than it would be if you applied for the same cover externally.

- *No medical examinations are needed.* If you are simply applying for the basic level of insurance cover that your superannuation fund offers, there are generally no medical exams needed. This can be an advantage if you might otherwise have trouble passing a medical with flying colours.

- *It can be tax-effective.* Paying for income protection, life or disability insurance within your superannuation can be tax-effective. This is because the premiums come out of your super account, which is taxed at a concessional contribution rate of 15 per cent rather than your marginal tax rate. (Income protection is also tax-effective outside superannuation because you are able to claim a tax deduction for the total amount of premiums paid during the tax year. Many people think this is only available to the self employed, but PAYG employees are also eligible for this deduction.)

Disadvantages

- *Generally the automatic level of life and disability insurance is a relatively small amount.* You may well need significantly more insurance than your super fund offers. Additionally, the income protection benefits may be limited to covering only a certain percentage of your income for a short length of time.

- *If you die, there could be a catfight!* Superannuation isn't part of your estate. Yes, you can nominate a beneficiary, as we discussed, but the final say as to who gets your money still rests with the trustees of the superannuation fund. It's a significant issue! Holding your insurance outside super gives you a lot more control over who should ultimately get the money.

- *Either way, there can be delays.* Because the insurance payouts have to go to your superannuation fund before they go to you, it can increase the delay in actually receiving any money. If there is some sort of health or family crisis (and let's face it, you wouldn't be making a claim otherwise) this delay can be incredibly stressful.

- *Beneficiaries could be taxed.* All insurance payouts that are made from superannuation funds are made from your pre-tax dollars. What this means is that if the funds are paid to someone who is not financially dependent on you, the money will be taxed, whereas the same funds paid in a policy held outside super would be tax free.

Step 5: decide how much to pay

Now, a detailed discussion of the benefits and disadvantages of superannuation as an investment vehicle is outside the scope of this 'money for nothing' book. However, it is worth quickly highlighting the two most common methods of boosting your superannuation balance tax-effectively. I'm going to assume that most readers of this book are either Gen Y or Gen X with 30-odd years between now and retirement and give a couple of examples of how putting extra money into super can help you.

Salary sacrificing

Basically, salary sacrificing is when you arrange with your employer to pay a portion of your pre-tax salary as an additional contribution into your super fund.

Pre-tax money that is paid into your fund is charged a superannuation contributions tax of 15 per cent, but if your marginal tax rate is higher than the contributions tax, then it's a tax-effective savings strategy. I'll show you an example.

Example 4.1: salary sacrificing

Assume that Noah earns $65000 per annum. He has a superannuation fund worth about $10000, with his employer making contributions of 9 per cent per annum. Noah is wondering whether to salary sacrifice $4000 per annum into his super fund. Table 4.4 shows his before and after situation.

Table 4.4: example of how salary sacrificing can boost your bottom line

	Without salary sacrifice	With salary sacrifice
Income	$65000	$65000
Less salary sacrifice	-	$4000
Taxable income	$65000	$61000
Less tax	$13050	$11850
Take-home pay	$51950	$49150
Superannuation	$10000	$10000
Plus employer 9%	$5850	$5850
Plus extra contribution	-	$4000
Less 15% contributions tax	$878	$1477
Super account balance	**$14972**	**$18373**

So, for a net cost of $2800 (the difference between Noah's take-home pay under the two scenarios) he has boosted his superannuation account balance by $3400 (which is $4000 less the 15 per cent contributions tax).

Government co-contribution

Paying extra money into your superannuation fund doesn't have to be done with your pre-tax dollars — it can also be done with your after-tax dollars. That's money you've earned and already paid tax on — in other words, any spare money, really, that you have sitting around. If you pay extra (after-tax) money into your super fund, it doesn't attract the 15 per cent contributions tax. One initiative that the government introduced a number of years ago is the 'superannuation co-contribution'. It's a strategy to help boost retirement savings for low- and middle-income earners. Basically (subject to an income test) for every dollar of personal contribution you put into your super fund, the government will match you, up to $1000. That's potentially $1000 of free money! It is subject to an income test which, for the 2011–12 financial year, is as shown in table 4.5.

Table 4.5: super co-contribution and income testing (from 1 July 2011 until June 2012)

Lower income threshold	Higher income threshold	What will I receive for every $1 of eligible personal super contributions?	What is my maximum entitlement?
$31 920	$61 920	$1, up to your maximum entitlement	Your maximum entitlement is $1000. However, you must reduce this by 3.333 cents for every dollar that your total income — less allowable business deductions — is over $31 920, up to $61 920.

Source: Australian Taxation Office <www.ato.gov.au>.

Depending on your stage of life there are additional tax-effective ways to boost your superannuation, including contribution splitting and transition to retirement strategies. However, any superannuation investment strategy should be done in conjunction with professional advice and is outside the scope of this book.

At the end of the day there's no one right answer to the question of whether or not you should be paying extra money into your superannuation; to a certain extent the decision will depend on your income level, your age and your stage of life. If it is something that interests you, seek out professional advice (try the Financial Planning Association and visit <www.fpa.asn.au> for a list of registered planners). Otherwise, the most important thing at the moment is to find the superannuation you have and to invest it appropriately.

So get to it!

Week 5

Indulge in a savings frenzy!

Seeing as how the past few weeks have been spent wading through the intricacies of insurance contracts and navigating government departments in order to track down long-lost superannuation (which, let's face it, doesn't really interest anyone) I think it's time for something a bit lighter. So, let's indulge in a savings frenzy!

This is the fun bit where you go through your budget (remember the one you put together in week 1?) and target a few areas for some concentrated saving activity. To make it easy I've already pre-nominated the areas as:

- electricity/gas
- water
- home phone/mobile/internet
- groceries
- two dozen extras.

Just as going on a diet isn't about cutting out all the food you love, reducing your day-to-day spending isn't designed to cut your fun. It's just about finding and getting rid of the sneaky love handles of fat in your budget that you probably weren't even aware of in the first place.

This week is very much self-paced because it's all about ongoing behavioural change, not just one specific task. In fitness terms this is the 'joining the gym and going every day' task rather than the 'running one marathon' session.

Step 1: cut your power bills

Electricity and gas are contentious areas these days, given that about half of the carbon tax–related price rises involve this essential service, so I'll devote a bit of time to it. Not that it takes a new levy to cause a blowout in our energy costs; in the five years prior to the carbon tax, prices in Sydney and Melbourne increased by about 60 per cent anyway.

'Electricity is actually made up of extremely tiny particles called electrons that you cannot see with the naked eye unless you have been drinking.'

Dave Barry

Nevertheless, it is an essential service — we can't do without it — so we need to look at ways to cut back. Here are some handy suggestions.

Switch things off at the wall

Okay, well, not the TV that's programmed to automatically record all your favourite shows, but everything else. According to consumer advocacy group Do Something, Aussies spend about $1 billion extra each year by leaving appliances on standby mode (that is, switched on at the wall). Being in the habit of switching them off is a *really* easy way to save money!

Turn off your lights

Being in the habit of switching lights off when you're not using a room or part of the house also helps. Energy-efficient light bulbs can save you heaps of money as well (if you don't mind dimly-lit rooms). The standard incandescent globes have been phased out, but if you're still using them, switch them over. The new energy-efficient globes use 80 per cent less energy and last about eight times longer. This equates to a saving of up to $30 per light bulb.

Adjust your thermostat

You don't want to be too hot or too cold — but some of us go to insane extremes when it comes to heating or cooling a house. A one-degree difference in thermostat setting can add up to 10 per cent to your power bill. Also, try using natural ventilation. In other words: open the window instead!

Wash in cold water

Your clothes, that is. And whatever you do, steer clear of the clothes dryer unless it's urgent. That one appliance can easily add several hundred dollars to your annual electricity bill.

Replace appliances wisely

If your appliances stop working, replace them with energy-efficient ones. To do that, forget the advertising hype of retailers and instead log on to the government's energy rating website <www.energyrating.gov.au>. On the website you can search for and compare pretty much any appliance you might need.

Compare energy providers

We shop around for our tradespeople, for our internet provider and for our phone services, but a lot of us don't think to shop around for our energy provider. Some states (not all) have privatised and deregulated their utilities, and consumers in those states now have a choice of provider. So if you live in the ACT, NSW, Queensland, South Australia or Victoria, then shop around! The easiest way to do it is online, via the relevant website for your state: MyEnergyOffers <www.myenergyoffers.nsw.gov. au> for NSW, Your Choice <www.yourchoice.vic.gov.au> for Victoria, QCA <www.qca.org.au/electricity-retail/ comparator> for Queensland, and Government of South Australia <www.sa.gov.au>.

Go green

According to government calculations, 92 per cent of the electricity used in Australia is generated by the burning of fossil fuels (something that will decrease over time). *But*, green is an option! Many energy providers give you the choice of switching to environmentally friendly power—check out the government's 'Green Power' website for more details at <www.greenpower.gov.au>.

Join the 10% Challenge

A joint initiative of CHOICE and Do Something, the 10 per cent Challenge was launched in June 2011 to help households save more than $2 billion a year simply by cutting 10 per cent of their fuel and energy usage. The website <www.10percentchallenge.com.au> has hundreds of great tips on—you guessed it—reducing your fuel and energy usage habits.

Step 2: reduce your water usage

After all the water-saving tips and publicity a few short years ago (which preceded the floods) most of us are probably quite good at saving on water costs by now. But in case you do still need some positive reinforcement, here are a few easy tips.

Turn your thermostat down

On your water this time! It's the easiest way to save money—ensuring that your water is not too hot.

Use efficient appliances

As well as checking the energy rating, when your appliances break down, check potential new ones for an efficient water rating as well. According to the government's Water Efficiency Labelling and Standards (WELS) scheme, over the next nine years we could save more than $1 billion by choosing more efficient appliances. The biggest savings are projected to come from installing water-efficient showerheads (compared with a standard shower head, a water-efficient shower head uses less than one-third of the water—a big energy saving!), using more efficient washing machines (again, a water-efficient machine uses only one-third the amount of water of a standard machine) and—umm—flushing the toilet less! Well, just using the half-flush. Go to <www.waterrating.gov.au> for further information. Also don't forget to check for leaks. One leaking tap can waste more than 2000 litres a month!

Other basics

Basics such as only running your dishwasher when it's full, adjusting the load indicator on your washing machine, and using your water waste on the garden will also save you dollars. Even turning the tap off (as opposed to leaving it running) while you brush your teeth can save you more than 10000 litres per year! Here are the estimated savings according to <www.waterrating.gov.au>.

Being water efficient

By 2021 it is estimated that using water-efficient products will help to:

* reduce domestic water use by more than 100000 megalitres each year
* save more than 800000 megalitres (more water than Sydney Harbour)
* reduce total greenhouse gas output by 400000 tonnes each year—equivalent to taking 90000 cars off the road.

Source: <www.waterrating.gov.au>.

Step 3: review your telecommunications

We love all our sources of telecommunications. We love complaining about them too, with the Telecommunications Industry Ombudsman receiving over 200 000 complaints each year. The main things we like complaining about are shown in figure 5.1.

Figure 5.1: top nine new telecommunications complaints, from January–March 2011

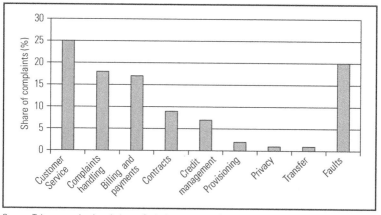

Source: Telecommunications Industry Ombudsman <www.tio.com.au>.

So, even quite apart from the financial aspect of it, it makes sense to review our contracts to make sure they suit our needs. And then, of course, there *is* the money side of it: heaps of money, potentially, can be saved in this area. Think how many communication devices you have—a landline with two or three handsets, a mobile, maybe a fax, internet, iPad ... technology is wonderful, but it does mean we're on call 24/7. And it can be expensive.

Sensible usage

Be sensible about your usage. Use a landline instead of a mobile where possible (and ask yourself how many landline handsets you *really* need). Make long-distance calls in off-peak hours; send an email instead of a text; stay within your internet download limit. And for goodness sake don't use global roaming when you're overseas. It's all commonsense stuff, but it's easy to forget.

For mobiles

Assess the plan you're on. Australia has one of the highest rates of mobile phone ownership in the developed world—we love them! So being on the right plan should be the first and foremost thing you do to save money on telecommunications. There are numerous providers of mobile phone services and literally hundreds of different products available. So, you need to know what your typical communication habits are, then find a product that suits your needs cost-effectively! In terms of your habits, ask yourself the following questions:

- Do you need a smartphone?
- How often will you use the internet on your phone?
- How often do you make calls?
- How many texts/photos do you send each day?
- Do you have a problem managing your phone bill? Should you consider going prepaid?
- Which contract time frame will suit your needs?

The way you answer these questions will help to steer you towards the types of contract that are likely to suit you. And once you have narrowed the field, try comparison site <www.phonechoice.com.au>. It's a great place to start your search.

For landlines

Weigh up your provider. According to the Australian Bureau of Statistics, the use of fixed or landline phones is in decline—but most households can't do without one just yet. Although there are not as many landline providers as mobile contract providers, it is still an open market. See what's available at <www.phonechoice.com.au>.

For the internet

The internet can be a minefield. Not just because of some of the freaky stuff that's on the www, but because of the sheer number of companies offering internet solutions. According to the Australian Communications and Media Authority (ACMA) there are more than 800 internet service providers in Australia. That said, Telstra and Optus are still the two most popular ones. When looking for an internet service provider, some questions to ask yourself are:

- How much are you prepared to pay per month?
- How important is internet speed to you?
- What usage limit do you realistically need per month?
- What level of ongoing service will you need?

Step 4: cut your grocery bill

Aside from your mortgage (if you have one) groceries are likely to be one of your next biggest expenses. We spend about 12 per cent of our income on groceries—not an insignificant amount. According to research by the Australia Institute, we *waste* more than $5 billion worth of those groceries each year. The report titled 'What a Waste—an Analysis of Household Expenditure on Food' calculated the cost of this wastage to be more than we spend on digital equipment such as flatscreen TVs.

Ironically, the food we *don't* waste is also very expensive for us in the long term: we spend billions on weight-loss programs as well! There are heaps of ways to cut hundreds of dollars from your annual grocery bill. Here are just a few.

Write a weekly menu

While it doesn't have to be set in stone, taking 10 minutes a week to write a guideline as to which meals you will have each day is a fantastic way to:

- save money
- reduce the stress of wondering what to cook each night
- give yourself the opportunity to regularly try out new recipes (because you know you'll have the ingredients).

Write a shopping list

Much of our food waste is because we buy items we already have at home and because we impulse buy (and eat) items we don't really need. Spending 10 minutes each week writing a shopping list based on your menu plan helps avoid food duplication.

Shop at ALDI

While it's definitely a 'no frills' service, a basket of goods at ALDI will cost you significantly less money than the equivalent basket elsewhere. CHOICE's Supermarket Price Survey (2009) found that ALDI is cheaper than the competition in all of the regions where it operates; on average it is 25 per cent cheaper than Coles and Woolworths. When you add up how much you spend each month on groceries, 25 per cent is a lot to save! The main disadvantage is that ALDI only operates on the east coast of Australia (at this stage) and that its product range is more limited than that of its competitors. Nevertheless, it should be possible to do at least three-quarters of your shopping at ALDI.

Shop online

If you can't shop at ALDI, consider shopping online if possible. Both Coles and Woolworths offer online shopping and while there is a small delivery fee, this cost is easily outweighed by the benefit of avoiding the impulse buys that we tend to grab instore.

Take your own bags

It might sound a bit silly, but taking your own shopping bags can also be a great way to limit your impulse buys because their finite space is self limiting. You can only fit so much into them!

Shop once per week

Apart from bread and fruit, aim to do all your shopping for the week in one hit. Making several trips to the shops is another sure-fire way to end up with heaps of items you didn't really want or need.

Step 5: choose some extras

Because I like to leave no stone unturned (that is, overload my readers) in the quest for savings, here are another 24 random cost-cutting possibilities—all ones that can save you money without decreasing your quality of lifestyle:

- Wash your own car. Unless some obliging school kids call in with a BYO bucket and sponge, getting your car washed can cost upwards of $50. It can be half an hour of good exercise for you instead.

- Wash your own dog. Doggie hydrobaths? Puhlease! There's nothing wrong with a hose and a towel and it takes no more than a few minutes.

- Take a cut lunch to work. You could save more than $1000 per annum.

- Surf eBay before hitting the bricks-and-mortar shops.

- Sell your pre-loved stuff on eBay, too.

- Use accessories to update your wardrobe rather than buying heaps of new clothes.

- Make your own 'takeaway' by cooking double portions of your favourite meals and freezing half.

- Give a slow-cooker a try. Seriously, some people swear by them.

- Avoid pre-packaged snacks. They're expensive and usually do not taste as nice as something made at home.

- Make your own cleaning products. Cleaning products are actually quite expensive. Making your own out of ingredients such as bicarbonate of soda, white vinegar, washing soda and borax, as well as lemon oil, can be cheap—and better for the environment.

- Buy generic at the supermarket (not always, but a lot of it is great quality).

- Buy generic at the pharmacy when practical. The same ingredients, without the branding, can be surprisingly cheap.

- Pay your bills on time. It's easy to lose track of when bills are due, but some companies have hefty late fees (and some also have discounts for paying the bill early).

- Plan ahead for birthday gifts. We're always lectured about planning ahead for Christmas—but the dozens of birthday gifts throughout the year can be a budget killer too. Plan ahead and give yourself enough time to buy things on sale or online.

- Use your local library: ebooks are cheaper than the printed version, but libraries are free (provided you remember to return the book/DVD on time and avoid a late fee).

- Join a toy library as well, if you have kids.

- Always ask for a discount when buying large items (especially if you are paying with cash).

- Grow your own herbs. Basil, coriander, parsley and mint are easy to grow. They look nice, smell great and taste even better.

- Look objectively at your memberships and subscriptions. I mean things such as gym and club memberships, and magazine and newspaper subscriptions. Be honest about whether or not you really use them.

- Look objectively at your bank account from time to time. Mistakes do happen — use internet banking every few days to ensure that all the transactions listed belong to you.

- Buy an espresso machine/juicer. If you love your daily coffee hit or freshly made juice, make it at home before you leave for work.

- Keep all of your receipts. We will spend a week focussing on tax stuff later, but the most fundamental thing you have to do to maximise your return is keep your receipts. If you don't have the proof of purchase, you (usually) can't claim it!

- Use your car less. Public transport, car pooling and cycling can all be great alternatives for getting from point A to point B.

- Check out the deals towards the end of year when buying a car, or when they are changing models.

I'm sure you could think of heaps more savings strategies. It's really only limited by your imagination and motivation!

Attack your credit cards!

We love to hate them and hate to love them, but for many of us credit cards are a fact of life. Sometimes a pricey fact—in Australia we currently owe about $50 billion on credit, three-quarters of which accrues interest. At an average interest rate of 17 per cent, that equates to billions of dollars in bank revenue every year.

So much bank revenue. I mean, why else do they have huge marketing budgets for their credit cards? Why else are there all those advertisements showing beautiful, shiny people buying beautiful, shiny things that apparently in some way make their life happier and shinier and, well, more beautiful? It's not for our benefit, believe me!

So, as consumers we're paying interest on somewhere between $36 billion and $40 billion on our credit cards. We get annoyed when the government runs a deficit—bad financial management and all that—but we're not exactly keeping our own house of cards in the greatest of order. The thing is though, that it's not in anyone's interest except your own to pay off your credit card. It's certainly not in your bank's interest, nor is it in the interest of retailers—probably not even the government's to a certain extent, because less spending means less economic growth.

You have to rely on yourself!

Not that you should be pocketing the plastic and sticking to cash—credit cards are incredibly useful. You just don't want to be paying interest on them. Or if you *are* paying interest, you want it to be as small an amount as possible.

> '*Overall, 30 per cent of survey respondents said that they always or often pay one or more essential bills using their credit card and then do not pay off their card in full.*'
>
> *The Australia Institute, 2010*

The thing is though, that between a new credit card here, a store card there and offers of limit increases arriving in the mail every other week, we can build up a mountain of plastic—and debt—before we realise it. It's very, very easy for it all to get out of control. And the biggest problem is that if you suddenly find yourself using a credit card to supplement your living expenses...then you're on a one-way ride to wage-slavery and all the stress that goes along with it.

Plus, those seemingly modest purchases can turn out to be really expensive! As an example, let's say you owe $5000 on your credit card (which is basically the average credit card balance out there). Maybe you used your card to pay for a trip to Fiji, buy a new bike or re-outfit your wardrobe and never quite got around to paying the balance off your card. At an average interest rate and making minimum repayments, that $5000 debt will cost you an extra $11 300 in interest before you're done, as opposed to just $1200 in interest if you got your repayment act together and put $200 a month towards reducing the balance. More than $10 000 difference in costs! If that's not 'money for nothing', I don't know what is!

In July 2012 the National Consumer Credit Protection Amendment will come into effect. This amendment is designed to help consumers better manage their debt.

According to Treasury the changes will:

- place limits on how much credit card accounts can go over their specified limit and abolish fees when they do so
- require credit card providers to allocate repayments to higher interest debts first
- ban unsolicited credit limit extension offers unless pre-agreed to by the consumer
- make it mandatory for credit-card application forms to include a clear summary of key account features.

It's all good stuff…but…at the end of the day the buck has to stop with you. So this week it's all about getting your credit-card debt under control—in three easy steps! Basically we're going to:

1 pay off your current credit card balances

2 change your spending habits

3 choose a card that's right for you.

It's not difficult to do (truly, believe me). So let's get started!

Step 1: pay off your debt

This is the most difficult step of all because it entails facing up to your spending habits—which many of us, myself included, don't like to do too often. Let's be realistic: if you have had an outstanding balance on your credit or store cards for more than three months, chances are—unless it related to one specific, unforeseen event—you are not going to pay it off. A consistently unpaid credit card balance is an indication that you are living beyond your means (and by the way, you're in good company: the government does it all the time). If you're already living beyond your means though, then the chances of reducing your living expenses sufficiently to live within your means *and* pay off a credit-card debt are pretty remote. In which case you need to face the facts and do something about it.

What to do? You need to minimise the impact that this debt has on your cash flow. That means refinancing your debt at the lowest interest rate possible and setting up a realistic repayment plan to get the debt paid off. There are three main ways you can do this.

- Incorporate the debts into your mortgage *and increase your regular repayments*.

- Consolidate your credit-card debts into one personal loan *with a defined lifespan of, say, five years*.

- Transfer your balances onto a card offering honeymoon rates *and pay it off*.

Let's look at the options one by one.

Incorporate your debts

You can do this by incorporating your credit-card debts into your mortgage. Of course, this only works if you have a mortgage and the available equity against your home. And — very important — provided your bank doesn't charge you any hefty fees for doing it.

If you can tick all those boxes though, then incorporating your debt can be both cost-effective and easy on your budget. Table 6.1 shows how much interest you would pay if your credit-card debt is separate from your mortgage.

Table 6.1: separate credit-card and mortgage debts

Type	Amount owing	Rate	Monthly repayment	Details
Credit card	$10 000	17.0%	$200	Paid off in 50 years at a total interest cost of $23 460
25-year mortgage	$350 000	8.0%	$2 701	Paid off in 25 years at a total interest cost of $460 407
Monthly repayment/total interest			**$2 901**	**$483 867**

Table 6.2 shows how much interest you can save by incorporating your credit-card debt into your mortgage.

Table 6.2: combined credit-card and mortgage debts

Type	Amount owing	Rate	Monthly repayment	Details
25-year mortgage	$360 000	8.0%	$2 901	Paid off in 22 years at a total interest cost of $406 757
Monthly repayment/total interest			**$2 901**	**$406 757**
Total interest saving				**$77 110**

As you can see from this example, incorporating your $10 000 credit-card debt into your mortgage and keeping your overall repayment level the same not only means you will eventually pay off your mortgage, but also means you can potentially save a whopping amount of overall interest.

As such, this is potentially a fantastic way to erase your credit-card debt. It does, however, only work effectively under these conditions:

- You have a mortgage.
- You keep your repayment level the same (that is, you increase your mortgage repayment to reflect the amount you were previously paying onto your credit card each month).
- You resist the urge to run up a balance on your credit card all over again.

There are some fantastic online calculators available to help you determine your individual situation; give the mortgage calculator on the government's MoneySmart website a try, visit <www.moneysmart.gov.au>. This is the calculator I've used this week.

Consolidate your debts

If you don't have or want to use your mortgage as a debt reduction tool, then another option is to consolidate your credit cards into a low-interest personal loan. A benefit of this strategy is that a personal loan generally has a defined lifespan. That is, your repayments are calculated in order for you to be able to pay the loan off over a certain time frame (such as five years). Table 6.3 shows the interest payable on a $10 000 credit-card debt at 17 per cent.

Table 6.3: credit-card debt at 17 per cent

Type	Amount owing	Rate	Monthly repayment	Details
Credit card	$10 000	17.0%	$200	Paid off in 50 years at a total interest cost of $23 460
Monthly repayment/total interest			$200	$23 460

In table 6.4 you can see how much interest is saved by consolidating the credit-card debt into a personal loan.

Table 6.4: credit-card debt consolidated into a personal loan

Type	Amount owing	Rate	Monthly repayment	Details
5-year personal loan	$10 000	10.0%	$212	Paid off in 5 years at a total interest cost of $2748
Monthly repayment/total interest			$212	$2748
Total interest saving				$20 712

So in this example, incorporating your credit card into a personal loan (and paying an extra $12 per month) will help you pay your credit card off (reasonably) quickly as well as saving you about $20 000 in interest costs. Another good option! Again, though, it's only effective if you avoid building up your credit-card debt all over again.

Transfer your balances

The final, and also very worthwhile, option is to transfer your credit card balances to a card offering honeymoon rates—and pay it off. Forget about mortgages and personal loans and simply transfer your credit card balances to another, cheaper card. Oh and pay it off, of course!

In the quest for your consumer dollar, financial institutions are often more than happy to offer credit cards at 'honeymoon rates' (that is, very low interest rates that convert to much higher interest rates at a later date). The companies hope, of course, that you will transfer your balance and then promptly forget all about it, thus enabling them to charge you exorbitant rates of interest down the track.

Credit card balance transfers: the tricks and traps

When you're constantly paying off your credit card but barely putting a dint in it because the monthly interest rate is too high, advertised balance transfer offers can look very attractive. Banks also use low balance transfer rates to encourage consumers to switch cards and hopefully stay with them forever. That's why it's important to get the best balance transfer credit card for your circumstances.

While advertised offers may sound appealing, there are some fish-hooks to avoid in balance transfer deals.

Fish-hook 1

Most lenders apply payments to the outstanding balance that has been transferred first, rather than the new spending, which is attracting a higher interest rate. This has been a bone of contention for consumers who can, unwittingly, rack up quite a debt unless they refrain from using the balance transfer card at all until the debt has been repaid in full. The financial industry has signalled it will change its repayment allocation practices to correct this—NAB has been first cab off the rank in announcing it will deviate from the current

Credit card balance transfers: the tricks and traps (*cont'd*)

industry standard and now allocate repayments to the highest interest rate first. All credit cards will be required to do this by 1 July 2012.

Fish-hook 2

After the advertised number of months—this varies from 6 to 12 months to life of the balance—all unpaid balances are transferred to the standard interest rate. It's important to know what this 'revert' rate is, as it can be as low as 10.49 per cent or as high as 22.49 per cent. As a general rule, before switching credit cards, consumers should know the promotional rate, when it expires and the rate they will pay after expiration.

Fish-hook 3

There are no loyalty points or interest-free days on the balance transferred. Interest is charged from day one on balance transfers.

Fish-hook 4

When transferring from more than one card, there may be different introductory rates. The fine print in some cards says that where you've made more than one balance transfer, payments may be allocated to the balance transfer with the lowest interest rate first.

Finally, several of the banks have useful balance transfer calculators on their websites. Even better is a balance transfer calculator that includes the introductory interest rate and term, the normal credit card rate, the annual fee and any balance transfer fee that may be applicable.

Source: CANSTAR <www.canstar.com.au>.

It's very, very important to be aware of the potential traps as outlined in the box. *However*, by having a set-in-stone repayment plan it is possible to use the honeymoon period to your advantage. Table 6.5 shows, again, the interest payable on a $10 000 credit-card debt at 17 per cent.

Table 6.5: credit-card debt at 17%

Type	Amount owing	Rate	Monthly repayment	Details
Credit card	$10 000	17.0%	$200	Paid off in 50 years at a total interest cost of $23 460
Monthly repayment/total interest			$200	$23 460

In table 6.6 you can see how much interest is saved by transferring your credit-card debt to a card with a honeymoon period.

Table 6.6: honeymoon-rate card

Type	Amount owing	Rate	Monthly repayment	Details
Honeymoon rate card	$10 000	1.0% for 12 months*	$214	Paid off in 4 years at a total interest cost of $816
Monthly repayment/total interest			$214	$816
Total interest saving				$22 644

* This strategy assumes that you continue to transfer your outstanding balance onto a new 1.0% honeymoon rate card every 12 months until the balance is paid off.

Again, a fantastic interest saving … with the only hitch being that you would need to roll your money into a new balance transfer each year for four years. This can play havoc with your credit rating. Alternatively, you could increase your monthly repayment to 800-odd dollars and pay it off in 12 months. Realistically though, if you could afford to do that, then you probably wouldn't have a debt to start with.

Whichever of the three options is the most practical for you, the important thing is to *do something now!*

Step 2: change your spending habits

Consolidating your debt and paying it off is fantastic! The only problem is that if you don't address the issues that actually caused the debt in the first place (that is, your spending habits) then chances are you will simply build up your credit card balance again and — *oops* — suddenly you have two personal debts instead of one.

'Of every $100 spent in Australia, nearly $3 ends up as underlying profit for the banks.'

The Australia Institute, 2010

So the next step is to change your spending habits. It doesn't have to be difficult at all, it just needs a little bit of discipline.

Look at your budget

You already have an absolutely accurate, totally kickass budget that you put together in week 1. So it's incredibly easy for you to have a look through it and work out exactly how your credit-card debt has managed to build up over time.

Pay the essentials first

When your salary drops into your bank account, use it to buy groceries and petrol and to pay any necessary bills (such as phone, rent, rates or insurances) that are about to fall due. That way you'll know how much money you have left over to play with. If you *don't* pay the essentials first, then what tends to happen is your cash gets spent and you run out of money before the next pay day. Suddenly the electricity bill is due and gets paid via your credit card. By the time you get paid again you've sort of forgotten about that little bill ... and it never gets paid off. So, pay the essentials first!

Leave your card at home

Learn to say 'no'! We do live in a world of instant gratification, aided and abetted by finance companies. After all, if you're not spending money, you're not a profitable customer for them. A lot of our spending on plastic is instant gratification stuff because it's just sooo easy (and fun) to do. But while you're busy sorting out your finances, it's a gratification that you can't afford.

Use internet banking

Sometimes it's those sneaky direct debits we've forgotten all about that put our accounts in the red. Get in the habit of checking your credit card balance *daily*.

Beware: credit-card cash advances can be costly

If ever there was a way to get into debt fast, it's by using a credit card to withdraw cash. Certainly, an instant cash advance is a way of getting hold of money in an emergency or when other accounts are empty but the practice is fraught with danger, particularly if you are making a habit of it. Why? Because interest on credit card cash advances is up to 10 per cent higher than your usual card rate—plus that hefty interest is charged straight away, almost as soon as you finish at the ATM. There are no interest-free days for you to repay the cash advance so you can really clock up some debt if you're not careful.

But wait, there's more! As well as paying the credit card interest rate on a cash advance, consumers are also charged fees. Those fees can be different for Australian and overseas transactions. It's normal for overseas cash advances to attract fees ranging from $4 to $5 as well as a fee paid to the owner of the ATM used. However, in Australia you can also pay a similar amount in transaction fees for cash advances. It all adds up, so beware.

Source: CANSTAR <www.canstar.com.au>.

Step 3: choose the right card

As I've already said, the credit card market is lucrative; there are *billions* of dollars in profit up for grabs each year. As such, it's also a competitive market, with hundreds of different credit-card options for consumers to choose from. The marketing teams of financial institutions go into overdrive when credit-card sales are at stake: Would you like a gold card? How about a platinum one? Would you like one embossed with photos of your own kids? Would you like it to come with a free magazine subscription, or membership to a wine society? Are there any other 'free' extras that would you like? All at no extra cost, of course!

That's crap! *Of course* you're paying for it! Whether it's through higher fees, a higher interest rate or a shorter interest-free period, rest assured that you are, in some way, paying for whatever ego-stroking 'benefits' your bank is offering you. And the really frustrating thing about most of these 'benefits' is that they really don't benefit you much at all. What would be of far more benefit to consumers is an easy-to-understand fact sheet showing them just how much that credit card might cost them if they don't pay it off each month.

This is not to say that you should never accept any of the benefits — but only if they work in your favour. The trick, in other words, is to choose a card that's right for you.

First, let's look at some of the main features that a credit card might have.

Free days

Generally, these cards have the greatest number of days in between purchasing an item and when you have to make repayments. They don't necessarily have the cheapest ongoing interest rate though, so they're most appropriate if you're a spender who pays your card off in full each month. A potential trap to be aware of with free day cards is that the 'days' are calculated as at the date your statement is printed, not on the date you buy the item. For example, if the month for a credit card with 55 days free runs from the first to the thirtieth of the month, a purchase on the first day of the month will have 55 days of free credit, but on the thirtieth it will have only 25 days. Another trap is that if you don't pay your card off in full for some reason, the fee-free days become null and void. It's easy to get caught out!

No free days

These cards have a low ongoing or initial purchase rate, but the interest will start accruing from the day you buy an item.

No frills

This is a basic, vanilla-flavoured card that usually has no annual fee, a fairly low ongoing interest rate and no bells and whistles. For people who do use their credit card but don't spend vast amounts, this is usually a good option!

Standard features

A bit like a standard mortgage, a standard credit card is a middle road. It's not the cheapest interest rate, but not the most expensive. There are probably some rewards or perks, but not a full range. Generally, if you pay your card in full and don't attract interest charges, but don't spend enough to justify a rewards program, then this could be a good choice for you.

Rewards/loyalty programs

We will cover rewards programs in more detail in week 12, but basically rewards cards offer you special rewards—such as cash or frequent flyer points—for using the card. Generally these cards have a higher interest rate and higher annual fee to cover the cost of the rewards.

Premium features

There are numerous premium features offered by companies; they can include purchase protection on goods bought by credit card, free travel insurance, extended warranties and in some cases concierge services. You are paying for these services though, either through a higher annual fee or a higher interest rate than you could otherwise find, so make sure your level of spending justifies it!

Once you've familiarised yourself with the main features, you have to look at yourself: what sort of person are you? To do that, ask yourself which of these personality types you identify with best.

What is your credit card personality?

Credit cards are tailored for different profiles, and what's ideal for one is disaster for another. The tips and traps associated with our four common profiles will help you choose the right card from the pack.

Habitual spender

Personality type: one who struggles to pay off the card and carries over the debt from month to month.

Tip: your best bet is to go for a low-rate card with a very low or no annual fee. If you can get a suitable card that offers instant rewards or discounts at places you regularly use, that's even better.

Beware: don't be swayed by cards offering big rewards as these usually come with big monthly interest rates and/or large annual fees.

Occasional spender

Personality type: a person who only uses the card for emergencies or seasonal spending, such as Christmas shopping, holidays or sales, then spends the next few weeks or months paying off the balance.

Tip: try to find a low-rate card with a low or no annual fee. Look for interest-free days but remember that they are null and void as soon as you fail to pay your full balance.

Beware: like the habitual spender, you should steer clear of high-interest rewards cards as the additional costs would likely outweigh the rewards benefits.

Everyday spender

Personality type: a person who uses the card for just about everything, such as groceries and petrol, then pays off the balance in full every month.

Tip: because you stick to a budget and are disciplined enough to pay in full, the interest rate is of little concern. Instead, look for a card that has a reasonable annual fee, has maximum interest-free days and a rewards program you're interested in

Beware: platinum cards have lots of perks, but many have high annual fees; make sure you will earn more than enough rewards to justify the annual fee.

Big spender

Personality type: one who earns and spends a lot of money on the credit card and nearly always pays off the balance.

Tip: look for a card that provides features and perks that you use frequently. These may include free travel insurance, concierge service and a rewards program.

Beware: all cards aimed at big spenders have high interest rates of about 20 per cent. Just a few missed payments combined with the high annual fee can negate the benefit you get from your rewards program.

Source: CANSTAR <www.canstar.com.au>.

Just as we discussed in relation to health insurance in week 3, shopping around for a credit card that's right for you can be as simple as surfing the net during your lunch break. There are some great online comparison tools out there, including: CANSTAR <www.canstar.com.au>, Money Zone or Mozo <www.mozo.com.au>, InfoChoice <www.infochoice.com.au>, and RateCity <www.ratecity.com.au>.

Choose one or two and give them a go. And of course, when you've found a fantastic deal, don't forget to phone your existing bank and see if they can match it!

Ultimately, good credit card use is about being realistic and understanding your spending habits. Having a card that suits your month-to-month spending habits helps you to save money *and* reap benefits. A win–win for everyone—except the banks!

Renovate your mortgage

All right, we're on a debt roll at the moment so let's continue! If you don't have a mortgage, you can skip this and give yourself a week off (although you can apply the basic principles that we'll be discussing to any sort of loan). Otherwise, read on!

Your mortgage is likely to be the biggest debt you will ever have. And it is mind-blowing just how much interest you will pay on that mortgage over the life of the loan. See table 7.1 for an example.

Table 7.1: interest payable on a $350 000 mortgage

Loan	$350 000
Term of loan	30 years
Interest rate	7.80%
Monthly repayment	$2 520
Total repayment	**$907 037**
Total amount of interest paid	**$557 037**
Total interest in today's dollars*	**$227 496**

* Assuming 3% inflation.

So, your modest $350 000 mortgage will actually cost you a total of $907 037 over the life of your mortgage—more than $500 000 of which is simply interest repayments. Ouch! Of course, it's not all doom and gloom because hopefully your property will increase in value by far more than the cost of the loan!

Even so, making a few simple changes to the way your mortgage is structured can save you *heaps* of money—and there is *no point* in giving the banks more of your hard-earned cash than you need to.

Thanks to the National Consumer Credit Protection Amendment, which was introduced in 2011, there has never been a better (or easier) time to research and switch your mortgage. Effective 1 January 2012, the amendment introduced compulsory, one-page key fact sheets for new home loan customers. See appendix E for a sample 'Key Facts' sheet.

While they are far from perfect, fact sheets do at least give consumers a basic overview of the interest rate, the 'all-in' rate (rate including other fees), the total cost of the mortgage over time, the features included and an indication of what would happen to your repayments if rates increased.

Ultimately though, it's up to you to get the best deal possible. It may take a few hours of preparation and research, but it can be incredibly worthwhile. To whet your appetite just a little bit, let's use the loan on page 91 as a basis and look at a few examples of how much you could save.

Example 7.1: change the interest rate, increase repayments, or do both!

In table 7.1 we assumed an interest rate of 7.8 per cent. Table 7.2 shows how a change in interest rate can make a difference. In this example, we will change the interest rate to 6.8 per cent.

Table 7.2: reducing the interest rate

Loan	$350 000
Term of loan	30 years
Interest rate	6.80%
Monthly repayment	$2 520
Total repayment	$689 746
Total amount of interest paid	$339 746
Interest saving compared to original	$217 291
Total interest in today's dollars*	$89 131

* Assuming 3% inflation.

Negotiating a 1 per cent lower interest rate and keeping your repayments the same could save you a huge $217 291 in interest costs, with a present-day value of $89 131.

Increase your repayments

If you weren't able to negotiate a lower mortgage interest rate, then try increasing your repayments. In table 7.1 the monthly repayment was $2520. In table 7.3 we will change the repayment to $2620.

Table 7.3: increasing repayments

Loan amount	$350 000
Term of loan	30 years
Interest rate	7.80%
Monthly repayment	$2 620
Total repayment	$819 845
Total amount of interest paid	$469 845
Interest saving compared to original	$87 192
Total interest in today's dollars*	$40 278

* Assuming 3% inflation.

So, simply repaying an extra $100 per month could save you more than $87 000 in interest repayments, with a present-day value of more than $40 000. Plus, as a bonus, your mortgage is paid off four years sooner!

Example 7.1: change the interest rate, increase repayments, or do both! (cont'd)

The nirvana of strategies! Under this option you negotiate the lower interest rate *and* slightly increase your repayments. As you can see in table 7.4, this will reduce your loan term by five years and knock $168 000 off your interest costs. Personally, I love it!

Table 7.4: reducing the interest rate and increasing repayments

Loan	$350 000
Term of loan	30 years
Interest rate	6.80%
Monthly repayment	$2 620
Total repayment	$655 935
Total amount of interest paid	$305 935
Interest saving compared with original	$251 102
Total interest in today's dollars	$134 568

I've used the mortgage calculator on the government's MoneySmart website at <www.moneysmart.gov.au> to determine these amounts. It's an easy calculator to use. Log on and try it out with your own specific details!

All right. Now that you know what we're trying to achieve, we can get started. The three main steps you need to follow in order to renovate your mortgage are:

1 decide what sort of loan you need

2 practise some negotiating tactics

3 make your loan work for you.

This week will take you a good three or four hours to complete. It's easiest to do it in stages over the course of the week.

Step 1: decide on a loan type

Just as there are different types of credit card, there are several different types of mortgage. If you already have a mortgage, you're probably well aware of this, but let's run through the broad basics.

Variable-rate loan

This is a loan with a fixed repayment period (often 25 years), where the interest rate will go up and down (vary) depending on, well, on what interest rates are doing. Variable-rate loans can be absolutely vanilla-flavoured basic (with generally a low interest rate but also no additional features such as being able to make extra repayments) or standard (usually with a slightly higher interest rate but more flexibility in terms of making extra repayments or redrawing money). Variable-rate loans are by far the most popular mortgage product in Australia.

Pros and cons of a variable-rate loan

Because variable-rate loans are for a set period of time, they give you the discipline of having to actually pay off your mortgage, which is great! A standard loan will also give you the flexibility of paying off your mortgage early and making both regular overpayments and additional ad hoc lump-sum payments. You should hopefully be able to negotiate a discount on the standard rate by shopping around. The biggest disadvantage is that, as the loan has a variable rate, your cash flow is vulnerable to interest rate rises. Provided you haven't overextended yourself in the first place though, that hopefully shouldn't be too much of a problem.

Fixed-rate loan

Again, this is a loan with a fixed repayment period but unlike the variable loan, the interest rate is fixed for a certain amount of time (usually between three and five years). Again, these can be basic vanilla or have slightly more features. Fixed-rate loans have not been particularly popular in Australia over recent years, mainly due to our low official interest rate, but this generally starts to change as interest rates begin to rise!

Pros and cons of a fixed-rate loan

The main advantage of a fixed-rate loan is that it gives you cash flow certainty. That is: you know exactly how much your loan repayment will be over the fixed term period. If you're a new home owner, or perhaps setting up a business, or you have some other significant demand on your cash, this certainty can give you great peace of mind. The main disadvantages are that fixed-term loans tend to be inflexible — and expensive if you break the contract! You also miss out on the benefits of any interest rate decreases over the time frame of your fixed term.

Revolving line of credit

This is the most flexible of all mortgages because it basically allows you to treat your mortgage like one giant credit card. Yippee — it's Christmas every day! In essence, a revolving line of credit loan sets you up with a loan account and a predetermined 'limit' that you can draw to. It is up to you to draw as little or as much of the loan as you need, and you will only pay interest on the amount you have drawn down. It is run like a bank account: you can have all your salaries and other payments credited directly into the account, and can pay all your expenses from the same account. Lines of credit generally have a variable rate of interest that is set at a higher rate than a 'standard' loan.

Pros and cons of a line of credit

Oh, where to start? If you are an extremely disciplined person who can absolutely control your expenditure, a line of credit can be a cost-effective way to go. It's highly flexible — you can pay in any amount you like (and withdraw any amount you like). The very significant downside though is that it has no finite lifespan (it can continue forever) and gives you very easy access to your money. This can result in you playing an expensive money merry-go-round.

While these are the main types of loans, there are also other home loan products that are marketed slightly differently from these options (such as honeymoon rate loans, basic no-frills loans, split loans and package deals), but they are all variations of the broad options.

Whichever way you go, making a decision on what type of loan is right for you will help you navigate your way through the hundreds of mortgage products that are available in the market. Consider the options in table 7.5.

Table 7.5: mortgage options

Type of loan	Certainty of cash flow?	Ability to make extra repayments?	Redraw facility?	Offset account, multi-product discounts, other benefits?	Comparatively low interest rate?
Basic variable rate	No	Probably not	Probably not	No	Yes
Standard variable rate	No	Yes	Usually yes	Can be negotiated	Can be negotiated
Fixed rate	Yes	Probably not	Probably not	Probably not	Probably not
Line of credit	No	Yes	Yes	Yes	No

Another way of saving is to upgrade your home-loan package as described here.

Upgrade your home loan and save

With big rate discounts, it's not surprising that package loans make up a large proportion of home loan business written by the banks, with about half of all home loans written as part of a package. The burning question is, does the interest rate

Upgrade your home loan and save (cont'd)

saving compensate for the higher fee? The short answer is yes, particularly if you are borrowing in excess of $250000. The annual fee is fixed so the larger the mortgage, the lower the impact this fee will have on overall cost.

How does a package stack up against stand-alone products? We compared a $350000 loan taken as a package against a standard variable loan and a basic no-frills loan. Credit card and transaction accounts were added to these last two home loans to make the comparison fair.

Table 7.6 is based on the average rates on a $350000 loan from the five major banks.

Table 7.6: comparing a package loan with stand-alone products

$350000 loan		Stand-alone products	
Costs	Package	Standard variable	Basic variable
Mortgage rate (incl. discount)	5.08%	5.78%	5.15%
Annual interest cost	$17780	$20230	$18025
Annual package fee	$350	$0	$0
Annual mortgage fee	$0	$100	$100
Annual credit card fee	$0	$50	$50
Annual transaction account fee	$0	$60	$60
Total annual cost	**$18130**	**$20440**	**$18235**
Annual package saving		**$2310**	**$105**

Package: yes or no?

The table clearly shows you're way ahead with a package loan. You will save as much as $2310 compared with a standard variable loan with separate transaction account and credit card.

Even taking a standard variable home loan without the transaction account and credit card will still cost you $2200 more than a package with the lot.

You'll also be $105 better off with a package than the no-frills loan and separate products.

Admittedly there are some people who just want the cheapest loan they can find and would not use the credit-card and transaction account included in a package.

These people may be better off with a no-frills loan, particularly for a smaller amount, if they are absolutely certain they will not need loan flexibility in the years to come.

Getting something for nothing?

Not many of us like passing up something for nothing. That's why a home loan package is so tempting.

Its main drawcards are:

- a standard variable mortgage for less than the price of a no-frills mortgage
- a free transaction account
- a free credit card.

However, it also offers loan flexibility and features that are hard to measure in dollar terms. If you're new to the home loan game, you're likely to be dazzled by lenders' advertised interest rates, not realising that other factors may come into play as the years go on.

For instance, if you pay extra into a cheap 'no-frills' loan and want to access that money, you may have to pay a fee every time. You may not be able to deposit a lump sum such as a tax return into the loan. You may not be able to get the loan paid out earlier by managing your money through an offset account; you may have to pay to switch from variable interest to fixed...and the list goes on.

If you are borrowing above $250000, upgrading to a package with its fully featured home loan will guard against being locked into a loan that may not suit your changing needs down the track.

Besides paying less than you would pay for a no-frills loan, you get a transaction account and credit card thrown in for free. Getting something for nothing is always a good thing.

Source: CANSTAR <www.canstar.com.au>.

Step 2: negotiate

As you can see from the Reserve Bank of Australia (RBA) graph in figure 7.1, housing loan approvals haven't exactly been shooting the lights out. So, a very important thing to remember when you go looking for a loan is that *you* are the customer. Unless for some reason you are a high-risk client, don't view it as the bank doing you a favour by letting you take out a mortgage. *You* are doing *them* a favour by placing your business with them. In other words: you are the one who is in the driver's seat. Which is not to say that you should swagger in and act like an arrogant git — they probably don't want your business that badly! The financial institution is probably prepared to negotiate though — that's an important thing to remember!

Figure 7.1: housing loan approvals

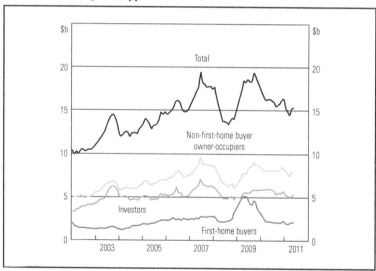

Sources: ABS and RBA.

Note: Excludes owner-occupier refinancing, alterations and additions and investor approvals for new construction and by 'others'.

Before you start shopping around, do some preparation to present yourself in the best way possible.

It isn't difficult stuff, it just entails the following:

- check your credit rating
- get your other paperwork together
- consider whether to use a mortgage broker
- find out what deals are available.

Let's look at each of these.

Check your credit rating

Have you ever checked to see what your credit rating looks like? It's something your bank will certainly do if you apply for a loan—so it's a great idea for *you* to have a quick look first, to make sure there are no nasty surprises.

Basically, your credit file holds details of all the loans you currently have. It also records details of any loan applications you've made (for example, credit cards, store cards) as well as details of some overdue accounts. It will indicate if you have been rejected for a loan in the past, and if you're a habitual credit-card churner it will most certainly show that. A bad credit history and bad creditworthiness can cost you a *lot* in the long term, so it's important to understand what is included in the report. The following information is from the Veda Advantage website.

How to read your credit file

A credit file includes information about you such as your full name, date of birth, drivers licence, gender and residential addresses and employer information.

A credit file has three distinct sections. These are as follows.

- *Consumer credit information.* This may include:
  - credit applications made in the past five years relating to loans for household, personal or domestic purposes
  - information that a credit provider is a current credit provider; that is, you have a current credit relationship with that credit provider (for example, a credit card or home loan)
  - details of overdue consumer credit accounts.

How to read your credit file (*cont'd*)

- *Commercial credit information.* This may include:
  - credit enquiries pertaining to applications for credit for commercial purposes
  - details of overdue commercial credit accounts.
- *Public record information.* This may include:
  - court judgements and court writs
  - directorship details
  - proprietorship details
  - bankruptcy information.

Overdue accounts

Overdue accounts may be reported as a 'payment default' or a 'clearout'.

Payment default

- A payment default is an account of $100 or more that is 60 days or more overdue. For example, if you have a phone bill of more than $100, and it was due more than 60 days ago, it could be listed on your credit file as a default.
- Payment defaults can only be included on your credit file if the credit provider has tried to recover some or all of the overdue amount. This means they must have sent a notice in writing to your last known address, saying that the amount was overdue, and requested payment.
- Potential credit providers may look unfavourably on applicants with a history of overdue accounts, so it's a good idea to avoid defaults getting onto your credit file. To do this, you need to ensure you pay your bills before they become overdue.
- If an overdue account is listed on your credit file, the credit provider is required by law to update the listing, as soon as practical, once you have paid the overdue amount.

- A payment default stays on your credit file for five years, even when you have paid the overdue amount. The fact that an account has become overdue and then been paid becomes part of your credit history.

Clearout

- A clearout is often called a 'confirmed missing debtor'.
- It means that, at the time of listing, the person who owes the money could not be located despite attempts to contact them.
- Before you can be listed as a clearout, the credit provider must make reasonable efforts to contact you, either in person (including over the phone) or in writing to your last known address, to pay the outstanding amount.
- If you can't be contacted, the credit provider can immediately list the debt on your file as overdue, even if it hasn't been overdue for 60 days or more.
- Clearouts remain on file for seven years from the date they're listed, even when you have paid the overdue amount. The fact that an account has become overdue and then been paid becomes part of your credit history.

Source: Veda Advantage <www.mycreditfile.com.au>.

Getting a copy of your credit file is straightforward: simply log on to <www.mycreditfile.com.au>, provide the personal details they require and request that a copy be sent to you. You can receive a free copy (usually sent within 10 days) or you can pay to have a copy express delivered. Once you have your file, check through it thoroughly to make sure there are no errors.

Get your paperwork together

Whether you utilise a mortgage broker or go straight to the lending institution, having all your paperwork together presents you as an organised person—and your chances of negotiating good deals are much higher if you've taken the time to tick all the paperwork boxes. So, grab a folder (put your credit file in it) and add:

- a copy of your balance sheet (you know — the one we put together in week 1)
- a copy of your budget
- copies of your bank statements
- identification
- a few recent payslips or your most recent tax return
- a property valuation (if you have one). The lender will also send out their own property valuer before they do business with you, but it can be useful to have your own independent valuation on file as well.

Showing the financial institution that you have put some thought and preparation into the whole process will hold you in good stead!

Should you use a broker?

According to the Mortgage and Finance Association, mortgage brokers now write approximately 40 per cent of all home loans in Australia. Given that there are literally hundreds of different mortgage products in the market that's not surprising: it can be confusing for consumers to wade through the bucketloads of information available.

Mortgage brokers generally offer lending products from a number (not all) of different financial institutions. Because they have access to numerous products, they will almost certainly have access to something that suits your needs and they can spend the time with you to understand what your goals are, to explain the options and to help you with the paperwork. They can potentially provide you with a very useful service.

Like any industry though, the quality of service can vary from person to person, so before launching into a search for product, the Mortgage and Finance Association of

Australia or MFAA <www.mfaa.com.au> suggests three main questions to ask a mortgage broker:

- Are they a member of the MFAA? The MFAA is the peak body for mortgage brokers in Australia and as a member of the MFAA the person or company you are dealing with subscribes to the industry Code of Practice, which promotes professionalism, ethical behaviour and transparency in all stages of the loan process you go through.

- What experience and expertise do they have? Don't be afraid to ask how long your loan consultant has been working in the industry or what their qualifications are. This person is going to help you make one of the biggest purchases of your life so make sure they are someone you trust and have confidence in.

- What are their fees and commissions? An MFAA member is required under the MFAA Code of Practice to disclose this information, and mortgage brokers in various jurisdictions in Australia are legally obliged to do so. Although there may be other fees payable in the loan process (for example, lender and government fees) the majority of brokers offer their service to the borrower free of charge as they receive their commission/fee from the lender.

To those questions I would also add the following two questions:

- How many lenders does the broker represent, and do they have a bias towards any particular lender? If they do have a bias, ask them why—it may be something as simple (and useful) as quality of customer service.

- What will your refinancing costs be? The refinancing costs are separate from the commissions that the broker receives. You have to make sure the costs associated with switching don't outweigh the benefits.

The communication needs to be a two-way street though; in order for a mortgage broker to help you, they need to understand what you're looking for. Is this a house you're planning on staying in for years? Is it a short-term stepping stone? Are you planning renovations? Giving your broker a sense of your future goals — not just your here-and-now — will help them match a product that will continue to suit your needs.

At the end of the day though, using a mortgage broker is optional and there's no right or wrong answer. Just do what feels right for you.

What deals are available?

Find out what deals are available either through the aforementioned mortgage broker or by doing some quick online research of your own, because there is no point in starting negotiations with your bank unless you already know what other deals are available out there. If you haven't already researched some options, it's difficult for you to be sure that the advice you're being given is good.

So — in the same way as you may research salary ranges on <www.seek.com.au> before approaching your boss for a raise or check out the accommodation deals on <www.wotif.com> before phoning a resort — check out what sort of honeymoon rates and ongoing low-cost loans the other financial institutions are offering.

The wonders of modern technology (and I love modern technology) mean that it's actually quite simple and quick to get a very solid idea of the deals available in the market — if only you know where to look. An online comparison site should be your first port of call. Try <www.canstar.com.au> and <www.ratecity.com.au>.

Having decided on the type of loan you want, you can refine your search. For example, your priority might be an excellent-value variable loan, or the lowest introductory rate in the market. Perhaps you want a line of credit with all the bells and whistles or maybe a mortgage that's fixed for three years, with an offset account included.

Home loans: try thinking outside the (four) square

During the global financial crisis (GFC) battering, the major banks grabbed even more of a stranglehold over the home loan market, at the expense of smaller lenders. Home loan market share is one thing, but product excellence is another and our research shows there is little correlation between the two.

While many home loan borrowers opted to go with the perceived safety of the big banks during the GFC, a lot of equal-quality or higher quality products were bypassed in the process.

It is true that competition is now active again — an encouraging sign for borrowers — and we've done some extra analysis to show exactly who is offering 5-star home loans.

Of the 130 products awarded a 5-star rating, mortgage managers and originators offer more than 46 per cent of them.

On the other hand, the major banks make up only 12 per cent of 5-star loans offered, but hold more than 90 per cent of the home loan market.

Smaller banks offer 9 per cent of our top home loans, ahead of building societies at 6 per cent. Credit unions add depth to this product sector by accounting for a sizeable 27 per cent of 5-star loans rated.

With so many outstanding products out there, why have borrowers been gravitating towards the big banks?

There are a couple of major reasons:

- Smaller providers just don't have the marketing dollars and can be easily overshadowed by the high profile advertising campaigns we see.

Home loans: try thinking outside the (four) square (*cont'd*)

- Lenders such as credit unions and building societies in general have more local focus in contrast to the nationalised approach of the larger lenders.

The bottom line is that prospective borrowers really should spend a little time researching available home loans rather than just grabbing the one with an attractive headline interest rate. There are various other factors to consider such as upfront and ongoing fees and the various features of a home loan.

Some institutions that may not be as well known as others still offer the same value if not better value products than those from the more well known lenders.

Source: CANSTAR <www.canstar.com.au>.

Basically, the mortgage features you're looking for can be specified and searched for—and compared against whatever else is in the market. Armed with all this knowledge, you are then in the perfect position to approach both a new bank and your existing bank to suggest they might like to match the deal. And if they won't, well, the deal is still out there for the taking!

Step 3: make your loan work for you ...

And don't overextend yourself!

Have a look at figure 7.2 to see what I'm talking about. Irrespective of whether you switch your loan or decide the one you currently have is perfect for your needs, the most, most, *most* important thing of all is to make the loan that you have work for you. By that I mean you should (within reason, because you need to enjoy your life) concentrate on paying off your mortgage as soon as possible.

Figure 7.2: household finances

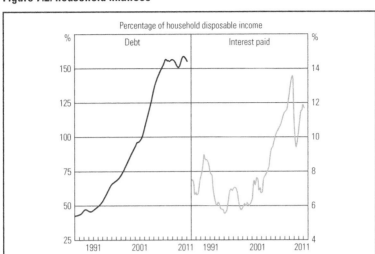

Sources: ABS and RBA.

Note: Household sector excludes unincorporated enterprises; disposable income is after tax and before the deduction of interest payments.

At the start of the week we looked at a couple of mortgage examples showing how fairly modest extra repayments can result in a huge saving. Now, let's look at a few more examples! So, as a reminder, table 7.7 is a copy of the original scenario.

Table 7.7: interest payable on a $350000 mortgage

Loan	$350 000
Term of loan	30 years
Interest rate	7.80%
Monthly repayment	$2 520
Total repayment	**$907 037**
Total amount of interest paid	**$557 037**
Total interest in today's dollars*	**$227 496**

* Assuming 3% inflation.

Increase your repayments

During the first few weeks we worked out our budget and identified some ways to save money. What if we applied that money to our mortgage? Let's say we're setting the ambitious target of an extra *$200 per month*. Table 7.8 shows what the result would be.

Table 7.8: increasing the monthly repayment

Loan	$350 000
Term of loan	30 years
Interest rate	7.80%
Monthly repayment	$2 720
Total repayment	**$760 006**
Total amount of interest paid	**$410 004**
Total interest saving	**$147 003**
Total interest in today's dollars	**$74 485**
Mortgage paid off within	**23 years, 3 months**

So, an extra $200 per month would save you $47 000 in interest costs (present value $74 485), and free up your cash flow almost seven years sooner.

Make lump-sum payments

If your budget simply can't support extra regular payments, how about committing to making occasional ad hoc payments instead? For example, when you receive your tax return, or perhaps when you receive a work bonus? Have a look at table 7.9 to see how even a once-off extra $5000 payment can make an impressive difference.

So, a one-off $5000 payment could potentially save you almost $49 000 in interest (present-day value $21 000). Not bad!

Table 7.9: making a lump-sum payment

Loan amount	$350 000
Term of loan	30 years
Interest rate	7.80%
Monthly repayment	$2 520 — plus an extra one-off $5 000 lump sum
Total repayment	**$858 101**
Total amount of interest paid	**$513 101**
Total interest saving	**$48 936**
Total interest in today's dollars	**$21 000**
Mortgage paid off within	**28.5 years**

Change your payment frequency

If you are currently paying monthly, consider halving your mortgage repayment and switching to fortnightly instead (see table 7.10). While this doesn't magically reduce the cost, there are 26 fortnights in a year — so it's really just a sneaky way of enabling you to pay more in without realising it.

Table 7.10: changing your payment frequency

Loan	$350 000
Term of loan	20 years
Interest rate	7.80%
Fortnightly repayment	$1 260
Total repayment	**$753 667**
Total amount of interest paid	**$403 667**
Total interest saving	**$153 370**
Total interest in today's dollars	**$80 403**
Mortgage paid off within	**22 years**

In table 7.10, $2520 per month would equal $30 240 per annum. However, $1260 per fortnight equals $32 760 — that's an extra $2520 paid off without you even realising it — pretty sneaky! Because you're paying more frequently (and because interest is often calculated daily) and as there are 26 fortnights in a year (not 24), changing the frequency of your payment can save you heaps!

Don't change your repayment

Rates go up and down all the time; it stands to reason that over the life of a 30-year loan you will experience plenty of interest rate fluctuation. When interest rates go up, we have to increase our mortgage repayments as well. But when rates go down, we don't have to automatically decrease our repayments. Out of sight is out of mind, as the cliché goes, and keeping your mortgage repayment at the same level after a rate reduction is a great way to pay extra off your mortgage without even noticing. So, for example, half a per cent decrease would look like the figures in table 7.11.

Table 7.11: interest-rate decrease

Loan	$350 000
Term of loan	30 years
Interest rate	7.30%
Monthly repayment	$2 520
Total repayment	**$774 391**
Total amount of interest paid	**$424 391**
Total interest saving	**$132 646**
Total interest in today's dollars	**$62 000**
Mortgage paid off within	**25.5 years**

And of course, increase your repayments over the years as your salary goes up!

Mortgages are a wonderful form of enforced saving. The more you save in those first few mortgage-owning years, the more money you will have to play with later!

Week 8

Personal insurance

This week we'll be looking at personal insurance, that is:

- life insurance
- trauma cover
- total and permanent disability cover
- income protection.

In other words: the stuff that insures you, personally. And yes, yes, I know — that's exactly where a lot of people switch off. It's boring. But it's also essential: having insurance can be the difference between a comfortable life or an emotionally and financially fraught existence.

What would happen to your partner if you died? Would they need to sell the house? Would they have to work longer hours? Would they be receiving bullying phone calls chasing payment of bills? (All while they're trying to grieve your loss.)

And what about your kids? It's enough that they would be having to deal with the loss of one of the main influencers and stabilisers in their life. Would they also have to change schools? Or be faced with having to develop a new peer group at a vulnerable time of life?

Surely they deserve better than that.

According to a 2010 ING report 'Picking up the Pieces', close to one in four children had to move schools within two years of the death due to financial pressure.

And what if you *didn't* die? Let's say you were badly injured, or developed a serious illness (cancer, multiple sclerosis, chronic fatigue, meningococcal—take your pick). What then? Who would look after you, and how would you pay the bills? Would your partner (if you have one) be able to afford to stay home and care for you—or afford the cost of a nurse, otherwise? Or what if it was you having to look after them? Could you do that *and* juggle financial stress at the same time?

Sorry to be so dramatic, but these things do happen. And while they are always going to be emotionally devastating, insurance can help to ensure that they won't be financially devastating as well. In other words, personal insurance is a risk mitigator: it can't prevent something awful happening, but it can help to minimise the stress that it causes both you and your family.

Personal insurance is something many of us don't adequately look into; we're far more likely to have our $30000 car insured than we are to insure our lifetime income stream (which for most of us will be between $1 million and $3.5 million). That's a lot of money to leave in the balance.

Eight thousand four hundred people aged between 25 and 49 die each year—an average of 23 people every day.

Let's look at it statistically: according to the Australian Prudential Regulation Authority (APRA), death and disability claims paid out for the year ending March 2011 were $4.46 billion. That's a payout rate of more than $12 million per day. Or consider this 2010 analysis.

Insurance: the payout figures

The Risk Store, which publishes yearly payout figures from the major life insurers, says that an average of $14.3 million was paid to 245 Australians every working day in 2010. That totalled $3.5 billion for 61274 claims.

The 2010 claims payout breakdown is as follows:

- term life: $1629150468
- TPD: $460736522
- trauma: $443736522
- income protection: $1033831983
- total: $3567649826.

These figures don't include all the vast amounts that are paid from superannuation funds' group insurance policies for 'early retirements' due to illness, injury and death, so the reality is much more than shown here.

The Risk Store says this is not a one-off statistic: over the past five calendar years the total from the retail companies has added up to almost $15 billion paid to policyholders.

That's a lot of people who never expected to claim — but had to.

Source: CANSTAR <www.canstar.com.au>.

Unfortunately, even those insurance payouts dwarf the total need, with 4 million people in Australia being diagnosed as having a disability — defined as any limitation, restriction or impairment that restricts everyday activities and has lasted or is likely to last for at least six months — in 2009, according to the Australian Bureau of Statistics 'Survey of Disability, Ageing and Carers' (SDAC). That includes around 665000 people aged between 25 and 44, and a further 898000 people aged between 45 and 59.

Death: impact on the family

Some key findings from a report commissioned by ING included:

- almost two-thirds (63 per cent) of respondents had less than a week's notice of their spouse or parent dying and almost half (43 per cent) found out about the death after the event
- 64 per cent of deaths were the family's main or equal financial provider
- close to one in four children had to move schools within two years of the death due to financial pressure
- almost one-third (32 per cent) of families moved house as a result of financial pressure
- more than half (56 per cent) went on fewer family outings.

Source: ING *Picking up the Pieces*, 2010.

As I mentioned earlier, even if you're young and single and can't see a huge need for life insurance, at the very least consider what happens if you *don't* die. A 2008 survey by the Australian Institute of Superannuation Trustees (AIST) and Industry Funds Forum (IFF) calculated that 45 per cent of workers were underinsured by $1000 a month for income protection. In other words, it's great to have car insurance and house insurance, but if you haven't insured your income and suddenly can't earn it, you may well face losing your house and car anyway.

So, *you do need personal insurance!*

This week we're going to discuss the following four steps:

1   the types of personal insurance available

2   where to get personal insurance

3   how to work out the right type of cover for you

4   the traps to be aware of.

You will probably need to set aside about two hours to work out roughly what level of insurance you ideally need and where you can turn to for personalised advice. So let's get started!

Step 1: types of personal insurance

Insurance isn't just insurance. There are several different types, all in some way designed to protect your finances in the event of injury, ill health or death, and the importance of each will depend on your stage of life. Specifically, there are four. Let's go through them.

Life insurance

Life insurance pays a lump sum of money to your beneficiary or beneficiaries in the event that you die. To that extent it's pretty straightforward. The purpose of having it is to ensure (as much as possible) that your family will still be able to afford the life you planned to have. That may involve paying off the mortgage so that there's no need to shift house, setting aside money for school fees or enough to invest so that the earnings will replace your income. Your family would go through enough emotional trauma if you were no longer here; life insurance is a way of preventing financial trauma from compounding that.

Changing school: impact on children

According to an ING report, of the children who had to change schools due to financial pressure resulting after the death of a parent:

- 69 per cent suffered from diagnosed clinical depression
- 75 per cent suffered depression, anxiety or panic attacks
- 78 per cent said their academic performance suffered.

Source: ING *Picking up the Pieces*, 2010.

Total and permanent disability insurance (TPD)

TPD pays you a lump sum if you become totally and permanently disabled and unable to work again. Policies differ slightly in what constitutes TPD; broadly it is when an accident or illness leaves you permanently unable to work again. Some policies define this as unable to work in your own occupation, whereas some have a broader definition as being unable to work in any occupation. There will be a minimum period of time — generally six months — that you must be incapacitated before your claim will be assessed. There will also be a number of medical reports required.

Similarly to life insurance, the reason for having it is to help maintain your lifestyle, adapt to new lifestyle changes and also help cover ongoing medical costs in the absence of your income.

Becoming disabled creates permanent change in family life. Your house may need to be modified for wheelchair access, you may need regular and ongoing rehabilitation therapy and regular care. While Medicare and private health insurance may cover some cost, there are certain to be extra — and significant — out-of-pocket expenses.

Trauma insurance

Trauma insurance covers you for a range of specified illnesses or medical events. What is covered will vary from policy to policy and may include up to 45 types of specific traumas (such as major burns, organ transplant or loss of speech), but the main events commonly covered are stroke, cancer and heart disease. Unlike TPD, trauma insurance covers you for events that, while potentially life changing, may also have only a temporary impact on your ability to work. The purpose of the insurance is to give you a financial buffer at a time of medical crisis. You may want enough to pay off your mortgage and to meet medical costs during your period of recuperation.

The cancer death rate

Cancer is a common disease and a major health problem in Australia today. At current rates, it is expected one in two Australians will be diagnosed with cancer by the age of 85. Cancer is a leading cause of death in Australia—more than 43 000 people are estimated to have died from cancer in 2010.

Source: Cancer Council Australia.

Income protection

If you are working, this is the most important insurance cover no matter what your stage of life. It's vitally important! How would you survive without an income stream? Centrelink benefits aren't that generous!

Income protection covers part of your salary (commonly 75 per cent) if you are unable to work due to illness or injury. You can choose a waiting period (the amount of time that you must be off work before you can begin claiming a benefit) and a claim period (the length of time that the policy will continue to pay you, which may be as short as two years or as long as up to age 65). The purpose of income protection is to provide you with a regular income during any temporary or permanent incapacity. And while it won't cover your full income, if you use it in conjunction with TPD or trauma cover it should be sufficient to maintain your lifestyle.

Research conducted by Rice Warner for the Financial Services Council found that more than half of Australian families would run out of money after only a single month without work.

Step 2: getting personal insurance

There are so many organisations! Personal insurance can often be taken out through your superannuation fund (which we discussed in week 4) or it can be taken out separately, through an insurance company. According to the Australian

Prudential Regulation Authority (APRA) there are 30 registered life insurance companies in Australia. As at June 2011, these companies are:

- Accelerated Protection by Tower
- AIA Australia
- Allianz
- AMP Life
- Asgard Capital Management
- Asteron
- Aussie
- AXA
- Bank West
- BT
- Budget Direct
- Clearview
- CommInsure
- GE Money
- Guardian
- HCF
- Insurance Line
- Macquarie Life
- MBF
- Medibank
- Metlife
- MLC
- MLC – Protectionfirst
- Nib
- OnePath

- Real Insurance
- Suncorp
- Swann
- Virgin Money
- Zurich Australia.

There are 15 friendly societies that also offer insurance:

- Ancient Order of Foresters in Victoria Friendly Society Limited
- Austock Life Limited
- Australian Friendly Society Ltd
- Australian Scholarships Group Friendly Society Limited
- Australian Unity Investment Bonds Limited
- CUA Friendly Society Limited
- Druids Friendly Society Limited
- IOOF Ltd
- KeyInvest Ltd
- Lifeplan Australia Friendly Society Limited
- Newcastle Friendly Society Limited
- NobleOak Life Limited
- Over Fifty Guardian Friendly Society Limited
- Centuria Life Limited
- Sureplan Friendly Society Ltd.

So, obviously you're not going to phone each company looking for insurance. As with all other financial products, online comparison sites can be a great way to narrow the search. In fact, nowadays you can even apply for life insurance online with a certain degree of immediate acceptance.

What is direct life insurance?

- Life insurance is death cover that provides a lump-sum payout of money on death or on diagnosis of a terminal illness that will end in death within 12 months. Direct life insurance is, as its name suggests, life insurance you can buy direct, either from insurance companies or financial institutions. There is no financial planner involved. The cover is easy to apply for, requiring nil or minimal medical information, and applications can be completed online, in the branch or over the phone.

- Some companies allow you to add other benefits such as total and permanent disablement, trauma and income protection using the same process. Sounds too good to be true! These products were designed especially for people who really should have life insurance but can't be bothered with the whole financial planner process. For instance, a new home buyer may decide to buy life insurance to protect the asset and ensure their family doesn't suffer financially, should the worst happen. As such, direct life insurance fills a useful niche that is becoming increasingly more obvious as its popularity continues to grow. Despite being only a relatively new product in Australia, direct life insurance opens up this sector and makes life insurance more readily accessible to a much wider range of Australians.

- With direct life insurance becoming more mainstream every day, how can you compare policies to see what's right for you? CANSTAR has undertaken an exhaustive comparison of direct life insurance policies to help you make an informed choice. We looked at products freely available to everyone; that is, products not restricted to membership of an organisation. We then examined features and pricing for different profiles and levels of cover, making our results more relevant for those making a short list of policies that may suit.

Why buy 'off the shelf' direct life insurance?

There are distinct advantages to buying a one-size-fits-all life insurance policy. In a nutshell, the benefits of direct life insurance are:

- it's much simpler to apply for this type of policy
- you can download the application form from the internet, or apply on the phone or at your bank or insurance company branch
- the questions are easy
- minimal to no medical information is required
- you receive a fast answer—you know straight away if your application has been successful
- you receive immediate death cover—you are covered straight away upon acceptance of your application.

These products appeal to people who know what they want and like the idea of having a straightforward life-insurance policy in place to protect their family and assets, should the worst happen unexpectedly. Direct life insurance is also a good quick-fix for someone who wants to put a policy into place straight away but plans to review their complete asset protection and investment strategy with a licensed financial planner a bit later on.

And the disadvantages?

Oddly enough, what makes direct life insurance so appealing is the very same thing than can prove a negative. Buying over the counter negates the need to see a financial planner who can assess your individual situation and advise on a product or course of action that you perhaps had not thought about. This can result in direct life insurance not necessarily being cheaper than a product that is more tailored towards your specific needs.

What is direct life insurance? (cont'd)

Because you are not consulting a planner and relying on their knowledge, you need to compensate and look carefully at exclusions in the policy before you sign up. Of particular importance are the definitions of pre-existing medical conditions. Some direct life insurance policies reduce the amount of cover as you age. All have restrictions on risky lifestyles such as working on an ocean oil drilling rig and motor racing in your spare time.

A financial planner understands what is covered and what is not covered in all the different policies and can steer you towards the one that best meets your needs. This is the trade-off you make when buying direct so it's really important to do your homework and make it your business to know what exactly you are signing up for.

Source: CANSTAR <www.canstar.com.au>.

Personally, I would strongly recommend that you make an appointment with a financial planner and get your situation sorted out properly. After all, it's potentially your family's financial security at stake.

Step 3: the right cover for you

It's beyond the scope of this book to give personal financial advice. You must view this insurance information and the sample calculations as general information only, designed to increase your knowledge of the issues. That knowledge is important though; before you get professional advice it's a great idea to put some thought into what insurance *you* think you might need. That way, when you talk with an adviser you will be able to actively drive the discussion. The Financial Services Council Lifewise project makes the following recommendations.

The right level of cover

Having the right level of insurance cover in place enables you to:

- *Preserve your and your family's lifestyle.* Life insurance enables you to continue to make mortgage, rent and other payments and can help you pay off debt. More than this, it empowers you to keep on doing everyday things such as spending precious time with family and enjoying the other things you love.
- *Stay in control and enjoy freedom of choice.* Some of the biggest benefits of life insurance cannot be seen and touched. Having sufficient funds to be in control during difficult times and having the freedom to choose treatment and lifestyle options is priceless.
- *Reduce stress and take better care of yourself.* Suffering from a serious illness or overcoming the death of a family member can be made even more stressful if you're struggling to meet your financial commitments. Life insurance can reduce your stress so you can focus on your emotional or physical recovery.

Source: <www.lifewise.org.au>.

So, let's look again at the types of insurance and some of the questions you need to consider.

Life insurance

The amount of life insurance that you will potentially need depends on your stage of life. If you are young and single, with no debts or dependants, you probably need minimal cover. If you are partnered with children and a mortgage though, your needs will be very different.

The main questions to ask yourself when deciding how much cover to apply for are:

- How much would be needed to pay out all my debts?
- How much would be needed to cover any other short-term expenses?

- What lump sum would be required to be invested to help my family maintain their lifestyle?

Total and permanent disability insurance

This also depends on your life stage, but this insurance does not have to be as all-encompassing of your financial needs as life insurance. That's because the assumption, if you're going to claim TPD, is that you are still alive and thus able to access your income protection. Some questions to consider though are:

- Will you have income protection as well? Or do you need the TPD insurance to cover your future income?

- How much is needed to pay out all of your debts?

- What amount might you need for one-off lifestyle modifications?

- How much is needed to cover any ongoing out-of-pocket medical expenses?

Trauma insurance

Similarly to TPD, trauma insurance is designed to pay off your debts and cover any large immediate expenses. Unlike TPD though, the assumption is that your illness or injury is temporary and that the lifestyle modifications wouldn't be as severe. So, some questions would be:

- How much is required to pay off your debts?

- Would you require a lump sum to enable your partner to take unpaid leave for a period of time?

- Would you require an amount to cover out-of-pocket medical expenses?

Income protection

Generally, income protection covers 75 per cent of your income (indexed) for a certain length of time. The two main decisions you need to make with regard to income protection are:

- How long can I afford to be without an income? This will determine your waiting period (the amount of time you will need to be off work) before your insurance payments commence.

- How long do I need to be compensated for? This will determine how long the payments last—typically you may choose a specific length of time, such as two years or five years, or nominate payments to continue until a certain age (such as 65).

It's a cost–benefit analysis: the longer your waiting period and shorter the payment period, the cheaper your insurance premium will be. But, you have to weigh that cost saving against the likelihood of needing to claim.

The Financial Services Council currently coordinates a 'Lifewise' campaign to help raise public awareness about the issues of both insurance and underinsurance. As part of that they run an insurance calculator to help consumers work out the approximate level of life insurance cover that would suit their personal needs. You can access their online calculator on the Lifewise website at <www.lifewise.org.au>.

I have used their online calculator for the following example focusing on Lisa and Tom who are both in their mid twenties. They earn about $50 000 per annum each and have recently bought their first home (a unit) together, with a mortgage of $280 000. They have a car loan of $30 000 and credit cards with about $5000 owing. Apart from minimal superannuation, they have no other assets and, currently, no insurance. They are focused on building their careers and on doing some travel over the next few years, and have big plans for a wonderful future!

Let's calculate Lisa's and Tom's insurance needs using the Lifewise website's online calculator.

Example 8.1: life insurance

Tom and Lisa have a mortgage and a car loan. If either of them passed away, the other would find it almost impossible to service those debts by themselves. For the surviving partner it would probably mean selling the home they had shared together and renting somewhere else at a time when they would be going through emotional turmoil.

They have no children to provide for, and presumably the surviving partner would continue to work. So, if their debts were paid off and funeral costs allowed for, there wouldn't be a need to allow extra money for investment. In that case, they would each need roughly the amount of life insurance shown in table 8.1.

Table 8.1: Lisa's and Tom's life insurance needs

Any dependants?	No
Debts to clear?	$315 000
Assets that could be sold?	$0
Current insurance cover?	$0
Expenses upon death	$20 000
Suggested level of cover:	
Life insurance	**$340 000**

Similarly to death cover, if you became totally and permanently disabled you would want to have the funds available to pay out your loans. At a time of huge personal stress you do not need financial stress as well.

Additionally, there may be one-off costs such as modifications to the house or car that would need to be made to accommodate the disabled partner. While ongoing medical care could probably be covered by a combination of private health insurance and income protection insurance, you might like to take some time off work, both to deal with the emotional impact of the life change and to provide practical support. If it's affordable, a year of replacement income for the partner, in order for them to take unpaid leave, is also a good option.

Example 8.2: total and permanent disability

Based on this information, the TPD calculation for Lisa and Tom would be roughly as shown in table 8.2.

Table 8.2: TPD calculation for Lisa and Tom

Any dependants?	No
Debts to clear?	$315 000
Assets that could be sold?	$0
Current insurance cover?	$0
Medical costs associated with TPD	$50 000
Replace partner's income for one year?	$50 000
Suggested level of cover:	
Lump sum to clear debts	$315 000
Other lump-sum expenses	$100 000
Total TPD required	**$415 000***

* With the assumption that appropriate income protection insurance is also acquired.

Similarly to TPD, trauma insurance is designed to pay off your debts and cover any large immediate expenses.

Example 8.3: trauma insurance

The calculation as to how much cover would be required for Lisa and Tom should they require trauma insurance would be something like that shown in table 8.3.

Table 8.3: Lisa's and Tom's trauma insurance needs

Any dependants?	No
Debts to clear?	$315 000
Assets that could be sold?	$0
Current insurance cover?	$0
Medical costs associated with trauma	$50 000
Replace partner's income for one year?	$50 000
Suggested level of cover:	
Lump sum to clear debts	$315 000
Other lump sum expenses	$100 000
Total trauma insurance required	**$415 000***

* With the assumption that appropriate income protection insurance is also acquired.

As I mentioned earlier, income protection generally provides cover for 75 per cent of income (on which, by the way, you will pay tax). The main two considerations are the waiting period (how long you could afford to be without an income before the insurance kicks in) and the length of cover (for how many years your income protection will continue to be paid).

Example 8.4: income protection

As Lisa and Tom have a mortgage and car loan to pay, and don't have any savings, they probably couldn't afford to be without two incomes for more than three months.

Because they are young, they really need a long length of cover as they have no way of knowing how long they might be off work. As such, they should choose a policy that covers them to age 65 (retirement age). So, their calculation could be as shown in table 8.4.

Table 8.4: Lisa's and Tom's income protection needs

Current income	$50 000
Multiplied by 75%	$3 125 per month
Length of time they could afford to be without one income	3 months
Length of time compensation would need to be paid?	To age 65
Current insurance cover?	$0
Suggested level of cover:	
Income protection to age 65 with a 3-month wait	**$3 125 per month**

Now consider the following ...

Time passes by. Tom and Lisa are now in their late thirties and have two young children aged eight and six. Tom earns $105 000 per annum now, while Lisa has cut back her work to raise their family. She works part time and earns $30 000 per annum. They have upsized from their unit to a family home and now have a mortgage of $220 000. They no longer have a car loan, but owe about $10 000 on credit cards.

Tom has a superannuation fund worth $85 000 and Lisa has a super fund worth $30 000. They also have around $30 000 in shares.

Their older daughter is at school and they hope to send both children to private school for their secondary education.

Example 8.5: life insurance and TPD with children

As you can see, their individual situations are now quite different. They have two young children to provide for who will have increasing financial needs going forward. Lisa has scaled back her career to raise their children while Tom is the primary income earner. The amount of insurance they need individually will be different. While their trauma and income protection cover needs would still be straightforward, it's worth looking at a new calculation of their life and TPD needs at this new stage of life. Tom may consider the sort of cover detailed in table 8.5.

Table 8.5: Tom's life insurance and TPD needs

Any dependants?	Yes — aged 8 and 6
Debts to clear?	$230 000
Assets that could be sold (shares and super)?	$105 000
Provision for children	$245 000
Replacement income for Lisa (a lump sum sufficient to replace Tom's annual net income until retirement age)	$1 300 000
Superannuation top-up	$180 000
Current insurance cover?	Nil
Expenses upon death	$20 000
Suggested level of cover:	
Total life insurance and TPD required	**$1 690 000**

Lisa, on the other hand, would have slightly different life insurance needs and she may consider the type of cover detailed in table 8.6.

Table 8.6: Lisa's life insurance and TPD needs

Any dependants?	Yes — aged 8 and 6
Debts to clear?	$230 000
Assets that could be sold (shares and super)?	$60 000
Provision for children	$70 000
Replacement income for Tom (a lump sum sufficient to replace Lisa's net income until retirement age)	$380 000
Superannuation top up	$51 000
Current Insurance cover?	$0
Expenses upon death	$20 000
Suggested level of cover:	
Total life insurance and TPD required	**$691 000**

As you can see, the addition of children and the change in their individual earning capacity has a significant difference on the amount of life insurance cover they need. This holds true at every stage of life. Every change in your life situation — whether it be a new member of the family, a new job, a change in address or something else — requires a reassessment of your insurance needs!

As a side note, in my years as a financial planner, a big mistake that I observed couples making was the assumption that the low–income earning or non–income earning partner didn't need insurance cover — because, after all, they weren't contributing financially to the relationship. What they were failing to calculate though, is the replacement cost of all the unpaid work! Who would pick the kids up from school? Who would do the housework, the cooking, the ironing? What if the surviving partner wanted to scale back their working hours to spend more time with the kids? These are all vitally important things to consider!

Now, your personal situation will obviously be quite different from the example I've outlined. However, it will hopefully give you an idea of some of the issues you can think about before getting professional advice. Don't hesitate to try the online calculator at <www.lifewise.org. au> for your own situation.

Step 4: beware of traps

When it comes to personal insurance, the devil—as they say—is in the detail. Leaving a section blank, ticking 'no' instead of 'yes', misquoting your income or forgetting about a long-ago medical condition are just a few of the actions that could result in a claim being denied later on.

In the 2009–10 financial year, the Financial Ombudsman Service (FOS) received 643 complaints in regard to life-insurance products—approximately 11 per cent of all disputes that they accepted during that year. One-third of the complaints related to income protection and one-third to term life or TPD. The majority of complaints related to claims being denied. The Financial Ombudsman Service sees this as a common problem.

A common problem with personal insurance products

A consumer has an income protection policy and makes a claim. Their insurer denies the claim because they believe that the consumer failed to tell them about a pre-existing medical condition before signing the insurance contract. The consumer complains to the FOS that their claim has been wrongly rejected.

FOS handles many insurance disputes like this. They are essentially about what insurers must ask customers and what customers must disclose to insurers before entering an insurance contract.

Source: <www.fos.org.au>.

There are three broad traps you can fall into when applying for personal insurance.

Non-disclosure

That's the aforementioned forgetfulness. It is so, *so* important to give the insurer all of the information they ask for in their application form: your *full* medical history; your *full* job description; a list of your hobbies and of sporting involvements; your family medical history. There are usually pages and pages of questions that you have to complete when applying for personal insurance. It's a boring task—but one that needs to be attended to in detail. The Financial Ombudsman Service advises the following.

Disclose all information

The consumer is required to disclose any information they know, or could reasonably be expected to know, is relevant to the insurer's decision about whether to enter the insurance contract. If the consumer does not fulfil this duty, the insurer may be entitled to refuse to pay an insurance claim or cancel the policy. However, the consumer's duty to disclose this information only applies if the insurer has asked questions to elicit the information, either in person, over the phone, via the internet or in a letter.

Source: <www.fos.org.au>.

Not reading the policy document

It sounds obvious—but many of us don't do it. Once you have laboriously completed the *War and Peace* style application form and have acquired the insurance, make sure you spend 20 minutes reading through the resulting policy document, just so you can be certain of the cover you have. You may have shopped around and considered a few different policy options: make sure you have ended up with the one you intended.

Not getting professional advice

I know: you've worked your way through this whole week. You've jumped online and played around with the calculators. You've surfed a comparison website to check out a few different product providers. *But*, you still need to get professional advice before you sign up for an insurance policy. Well, it's not compulsory but it's very, *very* highly recommended. Because when it comes to insurance, you just don't know what you don't know. Here are a few considerations.

- Does the life insurance have exclusions for suicide, or war? The latter is very important to consider if you plan on travelling.

- Does the TPD insurance pay out if you are unable to do your 'own occupation' or do you have to be unable to perform 'any occupation'? That makes a significant difference to the likelihood of receiving a payout.

- Do you need a buy-back option on your TPD or trauma cover?

- The specific definition of 'total and permanent disability' can vary from company to company. How does your insurer define it?

- Should you hold TPD and trauma as an extension to your life policy, or hold them in their own right?

- Should you take out basic trauma insurance (usually covering four or five conditions) or a comprehensive policy covering upwards of 20 conditions?

- Is your income protection an agreed value policy or an indemnity policy? It potentially makes a significant difference as to how much money will be paid out!

- Should you apply for a stepped or level premium? There are pros and cons of both!

These are just a few examples of the types of questions and issues a professional will go through with you when working out your ideal level of cover.

To get professional advice you can contact your super fund. In week 4 we discussed the pros and cons of holding insurance cover through superannuation. If it is an idea that appeals to you, you can give your super fund a call and make an appointment to see one of their advisers. Alternatively, you can see a financial planner. If you don't have a planner, ask friends or family to recommend someone. Otherwise, check out the Financial Planning Association's website: <www.fpa.asn.au>. You can use its website to search for a registered planner in your area.

Either way, make a vow to do it this week!

Week 9

Where there's a will...

Okay, so the whole estate planning thing isn't going to save you money in the short term (or hopefully not, anyway), but it's too important not to include in this book. We talked last week about some of the very real, very human devastation that could happen to you and your family without adequate protection. This is just the other step in that process. In the event of your death, a lack of estate planning can have horrible personal and tax consequences for your beneficiaries. In the event that you don't die, a lack of estate planning can have a serious impact on any business you may have, on your asset management and on your welfare in general.

Despite its importance, a heck of a lot of people don't bother to do any estate planning. Market research by Roy Morgan, commissioned by the Salvation Army, found that approximately 36 per cent of Australians aged over 24 do not have a will. The research also found, though, that 40 per cent of Australians aged over 24 (about 5.7 million of us) have experienced or know someone who has experienced family conflict as a result of a family member *not* leaving a will.

It's just not worth the risk of not having one; estate planning is dealt with under state legislation and if you die intestate (without a will) your assets will be divided up according to the laws of whichever state you were living in at the time.

That may be quite different from the way in which you intended it to happen—if only you'd written it all down.

So, while you ultimately need to seek legal advice to get your estate planning stuff in order, this week will give you a quick overview of what actually constitutes estate planning, and the issues you need to think about before visiting your solicitor. Please note though, that the information is very general and many details are not covered. You *must* get professional advice—it's a huge area!

There is more to estate planning than just doing a will! Sure, the will is a major part—it helps to divide your assets and nominate guardians for your children in the event that you die. But what if you *don't* die? What if you're injured? Mentally incapacitated? Who could make decisions on your behalf: run your business, manage your investments, decide on health treatment? None of us like to think about these possibilities, but they happen. And it's relatively simple to give them some thought and put some plans in place so that, if one of those 'what if' scenarios *does* unfortunately happen, it doesn't leave your personal situation in quite so much of a mess.

The major estate planning areas to think about are:

1   having an enduring power of attorney

2   having a will

3   writing an advance health directive

4   being aware of the stuff that doesn't go through your will

5   weighing up a pre-nup.

In step 6 I'll also give you a list of useful resources.

Your task this week is to read through all of the information, pick up the phone and make an appointment to see your solicitor. It's that simple.

So let's start at the beginning and work our way through.

Step 1: enduring power of attorney

Most people have heard of a power of attorney — a legal document that authorises some other person to legally act on your behalf with regards to your financial and property matters.

A power of attorney can be a short-term thing (you might, for example, give your parents a power of attorney to manage your banking while you travel overseas) or indefinite. An enduring power of attorney (EPA) has the added benefit that it doesn't become invalid if you lose your mental capacity.

'If you become unable to make decisions for yourself, without an attorney to look after your interests, you become vulnerable to people mishandling your assets. There may also be family disputes over your situation and how to manage your affairs.'

State Trustees Victoria

An EPA can be invaluable in keeping a business ticking along, for example, or keeping your investments running smoothly. It can be set up to take effect immediately, or to take effect in the event that you lose your mental capacity. Alternatively, you can nominate at any point for it to become effective.

Think about who to nominate

It goes without saying that the person you nominate to act on your behalf should be someone whom you trust implicitly! Also consider whether you want one or two attorneys. A few other considerations are:

- The person must be at least 18 years of age.
- The person must have the time available to deal with the practicalities of managing your affairs.

- The person should preferably be someone who is well regarded by the rest of your family.

- The person needs to be available and contactable, but it isn't necessary for them to live close to you, or in the same state.

- The person should be someone who will make sensible and considered decisions!

How to do it

You can either obtain an Enduring Power of Attorney Information Kit from your relevant State Trustee office (see step 6 for a list of resources) or you can request your solicitor to complete one for you. Personally, I always recommend going down the solicitor route. It's the type of document that you really don't want to stuff up through inexperience.

Step 2: making a will

'Where there's a will there's a way,' as the saying goes. And it's also true that where there's a will, that way can be a much easier path! Dying intestate (that is, without a will) is an almost sure-fire guarantee to cause delays and stress for your loved ones. A will simplifies everything!

If you die intestate and your only living relatives are more distant than cousins, the state government will receive your estate.

What is it?

Quite simply, your will is the legal document that sets out how your assets are to be distributed upon your death; that is, who gets what. It also covers some lifestyle issues such as nominating a guardian for your children in the event that both you and your partner pass away. Your will needs an executor (the person who will make sure that everything happens according to your wishes) and of course beneficiaries (the loved ones who get your stuff). You will also need a couple of witnesses to the signing.

Who will be executor?

Before you visit your solicitor to set up your will, it's worth having a serious think about who you want to nominate as your executor. Most commonly people choose their spouse or their adult children (an executor must be at least 18 years of age). But other popular choices are your solicitor or accountant, or a trusted family friend. Another option is your state public trustee office. Some considerations when you're making the choice include:

- *The age of your executor.* They need to be at least 18. Beyond that though, choosing someone who is significantly older than you increases the risk that they won't be around when duty calls.

- *The complexity of your situation.* Are your financial affairs limited to a house and two bank accounts, or is your situation quite a bit more complex? This could have a bearing on who you choose to administer your estate.

- *Your family dynamics.* Particularly (but not limited to) if you have a blended family, rivalries within the group might mean that choosing a family member as executor is impractical.

- *Whether you want more than one executor.* You can choose more than one person to be your executor— although having too many becomes a bit impractical. After all, they have to reach an agreement over every- thing. If you do have more than one, try to ensure they are people who will get along well with each other! Another option is to choose one executor, with a 'back-up' executor nominated in the event that your first choice declines or isn't available.

Who should be guardian?

If you have kids, this is a very important consideration. After all, your kids are worth more than all your other assets combined and your choice of guardian can make a huge difference to their happiness. So it makes sense to nominate a guardian as part of your will—otherwise it will be left up to the court to decide. Some of the things you will need to think about are:

- *Financial considerations.* Is it going to put your preferred guardian under financial stress to have your children? To a large extent this problem can be avoided by making sure you have sufficient life insurance available (remember we talked about this last week). This lump sum can be held in trust for the upkeep of your children, and managed by the executor of your estate (who is not necessarily the same person as the guardian). Don't be stingy with the amount—you want your kids to have access to all the opportunities that you would have given them.

- *Age considerations.* Is your preferred guardian too old/ young to be saddled with such a big responsibility? And is their life stage appropriate for both them and your children—not just this year, but into the future?

- *Lifestyle.* Will your preferred guardian be willing to instil in your children the values and outlook that are important to you?

- *Practicality.* It's not essential, but it can be a big help if your preferred guardian lives somewhere close by. Losing you is likely to be a big enough adjustment for your kids without the added upheaval of changing schools, leaving sporting teams and losing touch with friends.

- *Family considerations.* While many people choose a family member to act as guardian it isn't always going to be practical. Ultimately, the choice of guardian may be influenced by what you feel will be best for your child, irrespective of familial ties. Another important consideration is the competing demands of the guardian's own children: will the blending of the two families be practical?

It may sound obvious, but ensure that you ask the permission of whoever you do nominate as guardian for your children. If you have thought through the process then it's unlikely you would face a refusal!

Solicitor or DIY?

At a starting price of about $30, there is no doubt that using a DIY will kit is a cheaper option than visiting your solicitor. But is it a smart move? In 2010 the Australian Consumers Association (CHOICE) had four popular will kits evaluated (Will Kits, 24 March, <www.choice.com.au>). While they found them to be a good source of information, they also found significant differences in thoroughness between them. In all instances they concluded that with the right amount of knowledge and skills you could write a straightforward will using any will kit, but that they were not appropriate for more complex situations.

Here are some questions to ask yourself when determining whether or not you have the expertise needed to use a will kit:

- Is your situation in any way complex? We have already talked about simple situations (a house and a couple of bank accounts) compared with anything more complex. If your situation has a degree of complexity, you really should seek professional legal advice.

- Do any of your beneficiaries have special needs? Whether it's an intellectual or physical impairment or simply a spouse you don't like, there can sometimes be good reasons to limit direct access to your assets (most commonly through a trust).

- Do you understand the tax implications of your death? The transfer of assets to someone else upon your death can trigger taxation issues. In some instances the amount of tax will depend on how long you have held the asset, whether it was held jointly and who it is being transferred to.

- Is there any possibility that your will could be challenged? We all hate to think that our death could cause family division, but it does happen. Having your will prepared by a professional, with every 'i' dotted and every 't' crossed could help to discourage legal challenges. Personally, I believe your will is too important to be a DIY job and that a few hundred dollars is a very small price to pay for having your situation properly protected.

Step 3: advance health directive

This is one of the 'optional extras' that people sometimes like to include as part of their estate planning. Basically, an advance health directive is the document whereby you set out in writing your wishes for future medical care. Of course, if you have your wits about you at the time you are ill, you can make your own decisions at the time. The advance health directive, on the other hand, comes into effect in the event that you lose your decision-making capacity. You can nominate for the directive to come into effect at any time that you are unable to make decisions, or only if you are terminally ill. It can be a great way to help ease the decision-making burden that would otherwise fall onto your family.

Your solicitor can help you make an advance health directive, or alternatively the justice or health department of your relevant state government will have a form available.

Step 4: what *doesn't* go through your will

Not to put a dampener on all the enthusiasm that I'm sure you're currently feeling (because, you know, it's *such* riveting stuff!) but you can write the best will in the world and still not have everything covered. That's because not *all* of your assets are automatically dealt with through your will. In fact, some major chunks of your potential wealth are external to your will. The main exceptions are discussed here.

Some jointly held assets

If you have any assets that you hold jointly with someone else, those assets will pass automatically to the co-owner rather than through your will. So, for example, you can't bequeath your share of a jointly owned property, bank account or car; it transfers to the surviving owner. The exception to this is if you hold an asset as a 'tenant in common' instead. The difference between the two is that with a 'joint' asset you are buying the asset together and own half of the asset each. Under a 'tenant in common' arrangement you are each buying a share of the asset (which is not necessarily 50 per cent each) and hold those shares separately and distinctly from each other.

Superannuation proceeds

As we discussed in weeks 4 and 8, your super is not automatically a part of your estate. This is especially significant if you hold your life insurance through your superannuation fund (and in week 7 we discussed the potentially negative tax consequences of doing that). Just to reiterate, the payout of your superannuation—and any associated life insurance—is at the discretion of the trustees of the super fund.

When you join a super fund you're usually asked to nominate a beneficiary (the person or persons who you want the money to go to when you die). At the end of the day though, that nomination is simply a general guideline for the trustees to consider—it isn't necessarily where the money is going to end up. You can make a binding nomination (see week 4), but these have practical limitations as well.

The thing is, superannuation trustees are limited in who they can pay your benefit to. Under the relevant legislation, the superannuation trustees must pay the death benefit to your legal personal representative or to any or all of your dependants. The definition of 'dependant' can vary from fund to fund, but generally it includes:

- your spouse (legal and de facto)
- your dependent children (biological, adopted and step)
- anyone else with an 'interdependency relationship' (almost anyone, really, who relies on you financially).

These limitations are one of the major reasons why disputes about superannuation death benefits now total one-third of all complaints made to the Superannuation Complaints Tribunal. And it's a reason why so many adult (non-financially dependent) children are regularly disappointed in the decisions of the tribunal!

Death benefit distribution complaints comprised 34.5 per cent of complaints to the Superannuation Complaints Tribunal in the 2009–10 financial year.

The two main ways around this issue are to either set up a self-managed superannuation fund, or keep your life insurance separate from your superannuation fund (definitely a good option to consider).

Life insurance policy proceeds

Speaking of life insurance, an individual life insurance policy is another asset that doesn't automatically go through your will. Instead, you nominate a beneficiary and the proceeds are paid directly to that person on your death. Alternatively, you can nominate your estate as the beneficiary and have the proceeds distributed along with everything else.

Trust interest

Any interest you have as owner or beneficiary of a trust also doesn't go through your will. If you have a family trust, for example, or perhaps you hold shares in your business through a trust, the relevant trust deed itself should deal with how ownership will be transferred.

And finally, an important thing to remember is that marriage will automatically void a pre-existing will, unless it was set up in anticipation of the marriage. Divorce, on the other hand, *does not void* a will (although it can make some parts of it invalid). Just something to keep in mind…!

Step 5: weighing up a pre-nup

Well, if Kim and Khloe Kardashian both have them, surely they're good enough for the rest of us? Binding financial agreements (a form of which is a pre-nuptial agreement) have been legal in Australia for more than a decade. They are a way of allowing married, de facto and same-sex couples to detail in writing exactly which assets each person had when they commenced their relationship and how their financial affairs will be arranged if they separate. With more than 40 per cent of marriages ending in divorce, they can potentially be a great way to protect business assets, heirlooms and any other specific belongings that you treasure.

A pre-nup isn't necessarily set in concrete; a court will take into account how long you have been together, what level of assets you have built up over that time, and whether you have any children. All of these things can change the outcome.

Like pretty much any other legal document, you can ask your solicitor to draw up a pre-nuptial agreement for you or you can download a DIY kit online. As with pretty much any other legal document, my suggestion is to get it done properly with your solicitor. After all, a few wrong words or details through lack of knowledge could end up being a very costly mistake!

Step 6: resources

Estate planning is a very complex area—many books have been devoted specifically to it. That's why you must, must, *must* book an appointment with your solicitor. There are some great online resources available to increase your knowledge before you organise the paperwork, and the respective state public trustee offices are a good place to start. Table 9.1 is a list of relevant websites.

Table 9.1: online resources for estate planning

Vic:	NSW:
<www.statetrustees.com.au>	<www.tag.nsw.gov.au>
Toll-free: 1300 138 672	Toll-free: 1300 364 103
Qld:	**NT:**
<www.pt.qld.gov.au>	<www.trustee.nt.gov.au>
Telephone: (07) 3213 9288	Telephone: (08) 8999 7271
WA:	**SA:**
<www.dotag.wa.gov.au>	<www.publictrustee.sa.gov.au>
Toll-free: 1800 642 777	Toll-free: 1800 673 119
Tas:	**ACT:**
<www.publictrustee.tas.gov.au>	<www.publictrustee.act.gov.au>
Toll-free: 1800 068 784	Telephone: (02) 6207 9800

Now, pick up the phone! The best time to organise your estate planning is right now!

Week 10

More insurance

Does the whole insurance thing never end? There are just a few more insurances that you're likely to have and for which you could possibly be getting a cheaper and/or better deal. So, this week we're going to look at:

1   home and contents insurance

2   travel insurance

3   pet insurance.

Let's jump in and get it out of the way!

Step 1: home and contents insurance

Review your home and contents insurance: this is the biggie for this week and with a 2011 CHOICE survey finding premium savings of up to $800 for home insurance and $400 for contents insurance, it's well worth your time. You may not need both those covers, of course, depending on whether or not you're a homeowner; if not, then just concentrate on the contents part of it.

As I'm sure you know, this type of insurance protects your house and contents from burglary, vandalism and some natural disasters. Your chances of needing to claim aren't all that high—but when you do claim, it's usually for a significant amount!

It's worth reviewing your chosen amount of cover regularly as some insurers have an 'underinsurance' clause whereby if your home is not insured for current replacement cost and is destroyed you may only receive a part payout—a nasty surprise!

Types of home insurance

There is more than one type of home insurance. The following information is from the Insurance Council of Australia.

Types of home insurance policies

The Australian market now offers several different types of policy that suit a variety of insurance needs in the community:

Sum-insured policies

The total value of the policy is selected by the customer and determines the maximum available payout. With this type of policy, underinsurance can occur unless you diligently calculate the value of your assets. Some insurers automatically increase the sum insured each year to account for projected rebuilding cost increases.

Sum-insured policies plus margin

Some policies offer additional coverage above and beyond the sum insured selected by the policyholder. Additional coverage is generally in the vicinity of 10 to 25 per cent and can help address underinsurance issues relating to increased rebuilding costs.

Total replacement policies

Some policies offer total replacement for your building (not contents), reducing the scope for underinsurance. These policies require you to provide details about your home so that the insurer can assess its value. It is important that the representations you make about your building are accurate. Assistance in determining the value of your building and contents can be obtained from a variety of sources including tradespersons, building advisory services and consultants.

Source: <www.insurancecouncil.com.au>.

The more comprehensive your insurance cover is, the more it is likely to cost. So, the first step, of course, is to make sure you have the right amount of insurance to suit your needs and fit your budget.

How much should you insure for?

The replacement value of your belongings—and your house—can add up to a much greater amount than you might expect. It's important to be realistic about how much money that could be. As a quick exercise, take a stroll through your house/apartment and mentally note how much stuff you have. Try to tally up how much it would cost to buy new replacement items for all those possessions. It's likely to be a lot!

Likewise, with your house, construction costs could well be more than you think. There might be design costs, building application fees, landscaping and debris removal services. That's before the replacement building starts going up.

There are heaps of online calculators available to help you determine the appropriate amount of cover. Pretty much any insurer, in fact, will have an online calculator. Try the calculators on one of the following: Suncorp <www.suncorp.com.au>, Allianz <www.allianz.com.au>, NRMA <www.nrma.com.au>, GIO <www.gio.com.au>, CGU <www.cgu.com.au>.

Be thorough: put in all your details accurately and see what level of cover you ideally need.

Other conditions to be aware of

As with any of the other types of insurance we have discussed, you don't always know what you don't know. So, reading your insurance contract is vital—just look at the number of homeowners who were inadvertently caught out in the Queensland floods of January 2011.

Confusion about coverage is obviously a problem, with the Financial Ombudsman Service receiving almost 1600 consumer complaints in relation to home insurance last year, and another 560 complaints relating to contents insurance. The reason for the majority of these complaints was unhappiness about a claim being denied.

According to Geoscience Australia, floods, storms and cyclones account for 80 per cent of natural disaster costs.

When you are experiencing some form of crisis (and let's face it, you don't claim on your insurance otherwise) the last thing you want to find out is that you're not covered. While there is no definitive list of questions to ask your insurer (because everyone's situation is different and what might be important for you could be irrelevant for someone else), a few common issues to be mindful of are:

- What level of cover do you have? Is it a defined amount (which runs the risk of being underinsured) or a full indemnity policy?

- What types of natural disaster are you covered for? (Weather disasters make up the largest number of home insurance claims.)

- Do you have new-for-old replacement for your contents?

- Are accidental breakages covered?

- Is failure of electrical appliances covered?

- Does your insurer provide funding for temporary accommodation in the event that your home is destroyed? Otherwise, this can be a significant long-term cost.

- What will your excess be and what will be the progress of the claim if you cannot afford to pay the excess immediately?

- What other exclusions are listed on your policy?

Tiled floors are covered under home insurance, but carpets are covered under contents. A built-in dishwasher is part of the building, but a freestanding dishwasher is part of your contents insurance. An air conditioner attached to the wall is covered under home insurance but one attached to the window is part of your contents insurance.

How to avoid underinsurance

Just like sideswiping a Ferrari without having adequate car insurance (remember all the way back in week 2?) having your house burn down without having adequate home or contents insurance can be financially devastating for you.

According to the Insurance Council of Australia (ICA), up to 70 per cent of homes may be underinsured (that is, insured for significantly less than their replacement value). The ICA suggests the following reasons for this high level of underinsurance:

- *A gradual accumulation of possessions.* The number and value of things that we own can grow significantly over time; for example, purchasing a new television, appliances, furniture, technology items and clothing. If you add up the replacement cost of your possessions on a room-by-room basis, the total cost can often be a surprise.

- *Not accounting for upgraded assets.* Over time, people tend to replace household items and belongings with better quality and more expensive items. After a major renovation or upon upgrading your household items, consider whether your level of insurance should be increased.

- *Financial prioritisation.* Some individuals may choose a premium they want to pay and then live with an arbitrary level of coverage that this provides. This is not the same as working out the value of your assets and then insuring for that value.

- *Increased building costs.* The cost of building increases every year. New building regulations and bylaws may need to be complied with since the construction of your original building, adding further costs. You should also consider that after a major event impacting many households, trades may be scarce, pushing up the cost of your rebuild further.

So — as I have already mentioned — you *do not* want to be underinsured. Make use of the many online calculators available to help you work out what level and type of cover you need.

It's useful to know that there are ways to reduce the cost of your premium.

Reducing the cost of your premium

- Ask for a loyalty discount. Bundling all your insurance with the one company may entitle you to an even bigger discount on your cover.
- Choose a higher excess if you can afford it. Generally, the higher the excess the lower the premium. But remember, it's not worth having cheap insurance if you can't afford to make a claim.
- If you have installed security alarms, deadlocks or smoke alarms, find out if these will reduce your premium.
- Don't just pay your renewal. Shop around for a better deal. You might be surprised what you find.

Source: CANSTAR <www.canstar.com.au>.

When it comes to shopping around, you can access a full list of all authorised insurers on the Australian Prudential Regulations Authority (APRA) website: <www.apra.gov.au>. Alternatively, you can surf some of the online comparison sites available.

Step 2: travel insurance

Do you need travel insurance? Well, of course you do! If you're going to travel just about anywhere, you need travel insurance. Consider this rather stark statement from the Department of Foreign Affairs.

Why you need travel insurance

Each year we handle more than 25 000 cases involving Australians in difficulty overseas. This includes more than 1200 hospitalisations, 900 deaths and 50 evacuations of Australians to another location for medical purposes.

In cases where victims are not covered by travel insurance, such personal tragedies are further compounded by a long-term financial burden.

Hospitalisation, medical evacuations, or even the return of the deceased's remains to Australia, can be very expensive. Daily hospitalisation costs in South-East Asia regularly exceed $800; return of remains from Europe in excess of $10 000. The cost of medical evacuations from the United States regularly range from $75 000 to $95 000 and sometimes up to $300 000. The department has handled medical evacuations from nearby Bali in which costs have exceeded $60 000.

Unfortunately, not all of these cases involved travellers covered by travel insurance. *Travellers who are not covered by insurance are personally liable for covering incurred medical and associated costs.* As a result, we have known instances where families have been forced to sell off assets, including their superannuation or family homes, to bring loved ones back to Australia for treatment.

Source: Department of Foreign Affairs and Trade.

In other words, the government will help you find a hospital bed or a seat on a plane if you need it—but you'll be getting the bill in the mail! Don't risk it.

'If you can't afford travel insurance, you can't afford to travel.'

<www.smarttraveller.gov.au>

Many readers might not be aware of it, but the travel insurance industry is very competitive. An analysis by CANSTAR found premium differences of up to $940 for a single person with worldwide cover (see figure 10.1). That's enough for a return airfare to many parts of the world! As such, you can potentially save money by shopping around rather than simply taking whatever cover is offered to you when you book a holiday.

Figure 10.1: premium comparison—comprehensive travel insurance for a single person with worldwide cover

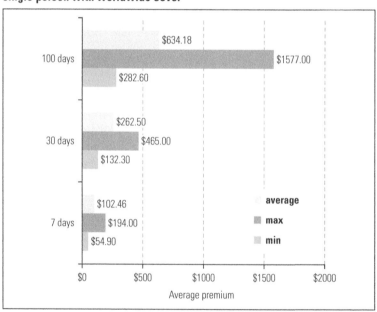

Source: CANSTAR <www.canstar.com.au>.

When choosing a policy, there are a few key things to consider:

- What type of travel insurance do you need?
- What are the possible traps?
- How can you make it cheaper?

Let's take a look at each of these.

Types of travel insurance

Travel insurance can be as basic or as comprehensive as you like—it depends on the premium cost you are prepared to pay and what personal risk you are prepared to take. Generally, travel insurance policies can cover:

- medical expenses
- disruption to your travel (for example, cancelled flights or personal illness)
- theft or loss of belongings.

Medical expenses should be a definite inclusion (if you don't remember the costs of medical evacuations, go back and read about them again). Whether you decide to cover disruption or theft will depend on your own personal assessment of the risk/cost tradeoff.

Possible traps

As for any insurance you need to—you guessed it—read the policy document! Each insurer will have different wording and different definitions as to what they will and won't cover. Fun stuff! There are a few common traps to be aware of:

- Some policies will refuse to cover you if any injury or incident occurred while you were under the influence of alcohol (or drugs).
- You may not be covered if the loss occurred as an act of war, terrorism or God.

- You will almost certainly not be covered if you travel to a country subject to an Australian government 'do not travel' warning. So here's an important tip: book your travel insurance as soon as you book your flight as most insurances will cover the cancellation costs if a warning does arise after you've booked. If you leave your insurance until the last minute though—you may be caught out!

- Injuries caused by participation in adventure sports may not be covered. Most travel insurances, in fact, will load your policy even for snow sports. So, if you're going on an overseas ski trip, make sure you specifically apply for a policy that includes snow sports!

- Failure to tell the insurer about a pre-existing condition could void your policy. It's always worth shopping around as different insurers will be prepared to cover different conditions.

- Deviation from your itinerary could cause the insurance company to decline a claim. Also, not all travel insurances allow you to extend your cover once you're abroad. As such it's best to err on the side of caution when you take out cover and buy a few extra days' worth—just in case of unexpected delays.

'Pre' can present a problem

In the insurance world a pre-existing condition represents an increased likelihood of a payout. This is why travel insurance companies are very particular about pre-existing conditions and the need for you to declare the condition upfront. Doing this gives the insurer three choices:

- to insure you regardless
- to charge an additional premium to cover the condition
- to decline your insurance request.

Definitions of pre-existing conditions vary but they generally cover the gamut of common ailments such as cardiovascular disease, diabetes and other chronic or ongoing ailments. These are detailed clearly in the product description statement each insurer provides.

Even though insurers do not like to insure pre-existing conditions you do have options. Before taking out travel insurance, read the PDS to see what they will cover and what they won't. If you have what they define as a pre-existing condition, phone them up and talk about the issue. Chances are, they will cover you for an additional premium. However, if they won't, there are plenty of other insurers out there worth talking to. Some even specialise in this particular area of travel insurance.

Don't tempt fate by not declaring any pre-existing condition. If your condition flares up or you become ill as a result of the initial condition, the insurer may void your entire policy. That includes paying for trip cancellation fees, accommodation—the lot. And, of course, no-one will even think about insuring you if you travel against medical advice.

Source: CANSTAR <www.canstar.com.au>.

There are a host of other possible situations. The Australian government has some useful information on its 'Smart Traveller' website <www.smarttraveller.gov.au>. Have a read before you start looking for a policy.

Make it cheaper

And now, of course, how do you make the insurance premiums cheaper? There are a few strategies you can use:

- *Increase your excess.* As with most types of insurance policies, increasing your excess (the portion that you will pay before you begin to receive any compensation) will lower your premium.

- *Consider medical-only cover.* If you are happy to risk the cost of theft or travel disruption, medical-only insurance can be significantly cheaper.
- *Enquire whether your credit card has automatic travel insurance.* Some cards do have travel insurance automatically included when you pay for your trip on the card. Cover is often fairly basic, but it's certainly worth checking out.
- *Ask for a discount.* It can work! Even if you're buying your policy directly online, you could try googling for a discount code—you might just get lucky! It's a quick search that could net you an easy saving.
- *Shop around.* Of course! There are more than 20 companies who offer travel insurance in Australia. The companies registered with the Insurance Council of Australia are:

  - 1300 Insurance
  - 1Cover Direct Insurance
  - AAMI
  - American Express
  - ANZ
  - Aussie Travel Cover
  - Australian Unity
  - Budget Direct
  - Bupa Australia
  - CGU
  - Chartis
  - CHI
  - Columbus Direct Travel Insurance
  - Good2Go
  - HBF Insurance
  - HCF
  - HSBC
  - ING
  - Insure and Go
  - insure4less
  - iTrek
  - Medibank
  - Mycover
  - nab
  - National Seniors

- NRMA
- Online Travel Insurance
- Ouch
- QBE
- RAC
- RACQ
- RACV
- Skycover
- Southern Cross
- Suncorp
- SURESAVE
- Travel Insurance Direct
- Virgin Blue
- Webjet
- Westpac
- World Nomads
- Worldcare
- Zuji

Additionally, you can use an online comparison site to help you find a cost-effective product. Try CANSTAR <www.canstar.com.au>, and Compare Travel Insurance <www.comparetravelinsurance.com.au>, or iSelect <www.iselect.com.au>.

Step 3: pet insurance

It's a bit left field — pet insurance is still a relatively new product in Australia. Having said that, it's certain to become more mainstream in the near future, with even Woolworths getting in on the act by offering pet insurance (among other products). And with a 2009 report released by Bankwest finding that Man's Best Friend costs an average of $25 000 over its lifetime — including veterinary costs of $450 per annum — it's a market ripe for expansion! While the report calculated average vet expenses of $450 per annum, more than 20 per cent of owners have had to spend large amounts of money on high-tech medical treatment (such as physiotherapy or chemotherapy) for their dog.

On their pet insurance information page <www.rspcapet-insurance.org.au> the RSPCA provides some examples of actual benefits that have been paid out to some of their members. These examples include the following:

- $918.80 was paid towards the veterinary bill for a dog who had lacerations from a fight.

- $3476.88 was paid towards a veterinary bill, courtesy of a motor vehicle accident.

- $1770.65 was paid for care due to gastric torsion.

- $232.92 was paid towards the cost of fixing a broken nail.

- $2535.87 was paid towards the veterinary bill to mend a fractured leg.

For many people, their pet is an integral part of the family. The idea of having the animal euthanised because emergency treatment is too expensive would be traumatic. Pet insurance can help give some peace of mind.

Types of cover

There are three broad types of pet insurance:

- *Accident-only cover.* This is the cheapest form of cover, but will only contribute to the medical costs if the injury was caused by an accident.

- *Accident and illness cover.* This is a more comprehensive insurance, which will contribute towards both injuries caused by accidents and the medical costs associated with illness. Dogs, for example, suffer a number of the same cancers as humans.

- *Accident, illness and routine treatment cover.* The most comprehensive, this covers everything already mentioned and also contributes towards routine treatments such as vaccinations.

Obviously, the more comprehensive the cover the more expensive it will be.

Questions to ask

As with every other type of insurance, there will be exclusions, loadings and limited benefits. A few questions to consider are:

- Is there an age limit for insurance? Some companies will only allow you to insure a pet between certain ages, or may restrict the benefit payout for older animals.

- What is the excess? As always, the higher the excess, the lower the premium.

- What conditions are excluded? Even with the most comprehensive policy, you might find that certain conditions (pregnancy, for example, or pre-existing or genetic conditions) are excluded.

- Is there a capped benefit? That is, is there a maximum amount the insurer will pay out for a particular illness or injury?

How to shop around

Shopping around for pet insurance is a bit more difficult than for most other insurances as it's a relatively new product and is not regulated in the same way as personal or general insurance. As policies can vary by one hundred dollars per annum though, it's worth the time. There are a couple of things you can try:

- *The direct route.* Petsure is a pet insurance administrator and underwriter, providing services to many of the pet-insurance businesses in Australia. Its website <www.petsure.com.au> has links to the various insurance companies.

- *Your own general insurer.* Some companies that offer home and contents policies also allow you to add on pet insurance at a very competitive price. So, give your insurance company a call!

- *Your health insurer.* Likewise, some health insurers also offer pet insurance, which can be either added to your policy or taken out separately.

  RSPCA Australia research has shown that pet owners are generally healthier and happier than non–pet owners. They have lower blood pressure and cholesterol; are less depressed; are at lower risk of heart disease; feel less lonely than non–pet owners; and actually find it easier to get to know people.

Week 11

Tax stuff

Many of us could save a huge amount of money if we kept receipts and claimed all our tax deductions. In fact, in my professional experience, most workers could save at least an additional $1000 simply by being thorough when it comes to doing their tax. Yet, interestingly, saving money by doing our tax thoroughly is rarely on the radar. A survey by The Australia Institute on behalf of Citi Australia ('Evidence versus Emotion: How Do We Really Make Financial Decisions?', December 2010) asked respondents what action they would take to save $5 per week. More than one-quarter of people would change bank accounts to save fees, or change electricity providers to save costs. Superannuation and mobile phone contracts were also popular, but no mention of tax (see figure 11.1, overleaf).

Yet, being thorough with regard to claiming all of our tax deductions can potentially net us a tidy sum of money each year—for very little effort! One example: according to the Productivity Commission, Australians donate almost $6 billion per annum to registered charities—but we only claim about $1.8 billion of that. There are at least a couple of billion in lost tax deductions right there! And after a decade as a financial planner, I feel confident in saying that there are undoubtedly numerous other ways for many of us to reduce our tax bill or get a better refund, if only we took the time to file all our paperwork properly.

Figure 11.1: action people are willing to take to save $5 per week

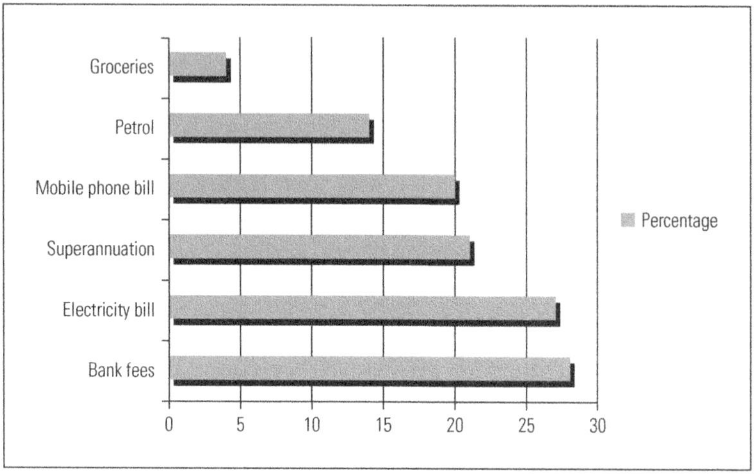

Source: The Australia Institute.

The Australian Taxation office (ATO) is 100 years old. Over that time it has grown from an organisation of 105 staff assessing 15000 tax returns, to one with about 22000 employees assessing more than 14 million tax returns!

This week we'll complete the following steps:

1   Do a quick overview of our income tax system.

2   Look at some of the common deductions.

3   Put some good tax habits in place.

4   Be aware of a few other tips and traps.

So let's get started.

Step 1: a quick overview

I should stress that this is a very quick and basic overview of our income tax system. After all, there are more than 5700 pages of income tax law—about 24 times as many as this book! And the tax-law pages are much bigger than mine! But all you need for the purposes of this 'saving-money-on-tax' topic is a very general overview of how the income tax part of our tax system works.

We get taxed on the income we earn. Whether that income is from paid employment, from running our own business, from investments or from Centrelink payments we need to pay tax on it. We also pay tax on the profit we make from buying and selling investments (capital gains tax) and on some fringe benefits that our employer may give us, as well as any income from trusts that we may be a member of. A few lesser known sources of income that are taxed are income protection insurance payments (if you have claimed on your income protection policy) and any other payments that are compensating you for lost income, as well as discounted share options.

What isn't taxed?

One-off payments that aren't associated with our regular income may be exempt, for example, a lottery win (provided you're not a professional gambler!). Some Centrelink benefits and some pensions are not taxable, as well as the odd garage sale or item sold on eBay and the sale of personal assets (such as your home). For pretty much everything else though—the government wants its share!

The government doesn't just take tax from our whole income though. First it allows us to deduct any expenses we have had to pay in the course of earning that income. (Well, not *all* expenses, but quite a few.) It also wants to encourage us to be responsible and healthy corporate citizens, so it gives us benefits for making a donation to charities, for supporting our family, for putting money away for our retirement and for excessive out-of-pocket medical expenses... and a few other things.

So, once the ATO has looked at our income, subtracted whatever deductions we are allowed to make and calculated the end result, it taxes us on that result.

In the 2009–10 tax year, individuals paid about $104 billion in tax.

In Australia we pay tax on a progressive scale; that is, the more you earn the higher the percentage you are required to pay in tax. The current income tax rates are as shown in table 11.1.

Table 11.1: tax rates for 2011–12 that apply from 1 July 2011

Taxable income	Tax on this income
0–$6 000	Nil
$6 001–$37 000	15c for each $1 over $6 000
$37 001–$80 000	$4650 plus 30c for each $1 over $37 000
$80 001–$180 000	$17 550 plus 37c for each $1 over $80 000
$180 001 and over	$54 550 plus 45c for each $1 over $180 000

Note: Plus Medicare levy of 1.5%.

The tax scale going forward will be as shown in table 11.2.

Table 11.2: tax rates for 2012–13

Taxable income	Tax on this income
0–$18 200	Nil
$18 201–$37 000	19c for each $1 over $18 200
$37 001–$80 000	$3572 plus 32.5c for each $1 over $37 000
$80 001–$180 000	$17 547 plus 37c for each $1 over $80 000
$180 001 and over	$54 547 plus 45c for each $1 over $180 000

Note: Plus Medicare levy of 1.5%.

That tax is then used by the government for the benefit of everyone.

Each year the ATO matches more than 500 million pieces of information, so if you forget to include something in your tax return, it is more than likely to be picked up when you lodge.

Step 2: common deductions

Okay, so even with a very general overview of the system, it's easy to see that the simplest way you can save money via tax is to make sure you're claiming as many deductions as you're entitled to. (There is also, of course, the opportunity for tax-effective investments, but that's outside the scope of this book.) Here are some of the common deductions.

Work-related deductions

About 65 per cent of individual taxpayers claim work-related deductions—they are, understandably, the most popular type of tax deduction. In part, what you can claim will depend on what job you do. Hairdressers, for example, can claim the cost of hair care products; airline cabin crew can claim the cost of rehydrating moisturiser; engineers can claim the cost of science calculators.

However, there are some common work-related deductions, which include:

- *Income protection insurance.* The premiums on your income protection insurance (remember we discussed income protection insurance in week 8?) are a tax deduction. The premiums for life insurance, total and permanent disability and trauma insurance are not.

- *Car expenses.* If you use your car for work—not just for getting to and from work, but any other work-related trips—then you may be able to claim some of your car expenses as a tax deduction.

- *Other travel expenses.* If you have to fly (or drive!) inter-state, stay overnight somewhere or catch taxis from place to place as part of your work, these costs are deductible.

- *Self-education expenses.* If the course you are doing relates to your current employment, you may claim them.

- *A laptop.* If you use it for work, you may claim the expenses.

- *A briefcase, laptop bag or electronic diary.* If you can substantiate that you need them for your role, you may be able to claim their cost.

- *Purchasing and cleaning work clothing.* If wearing a uniform is part of your role, the expenses may be claimed.

- *Depreciation.* If you own valuable work-related items that decrease in value, you may be able to claim depreciation.

There are many other work-related expenses, depending on the job you do. The ATO produces a set of fact sheets for specific occupations—you can check them out at <www. ato.gov.au>.

Deductions for study expenses

If you received Austudy, ABSTUDY or Youth Allowance you can claim a deduction for study expenses, including:

- the cost of text books
- home study expenses
- the decline in value of your computer (you can only claim the study-related proportion, not the proportion used for private purposes).

Make sure you retain your receipts in case the ATO asks you to provide them at a later date.

Source: <www.ato.com.au>.

Investment-related deductions

As well as work-related expenses, you can also claim a deduction for some of the expenses associated with your investments. These include:

- *Management fees on your investments.* Fund managers may deduct management fees from the funds you have invested with them—these are a tax deduction. Bank fees may also be a tax deduction!

- *Ongoing professional advice.* Whether it's from your financial planner, your accountant or your legal adviser, professional advice that is sought during the process of earning an income is generally tax deductible.

- *Depreciation.* This is generally associated with investment properties; you are sometimes able to claim depreciation on fixtures and fittings. In fact, there are a whole range of possible tax deductions associated with investment property, including insurances, rates, maintenance, land tax, gardening and cleaning, property agent fees … This is a specialised area and you should certainly seek professional advice.

- *Borrowing costs.* If you have borrowed money for investment purposes you may be able to claim the interest costs of those borrowings as a tax deduction.

- *Work or investment-related phone calls.*

Other deductions

- You can claim *up to $300 of work-related expenses* without the need to have written receipts. However, once your claim exceeds $300 you must have receipts for the full amount.

- *The cost of having your tax returns prepared* is also a tax deduction!

- *Donations to a registered charity*: Any donation over two dollars is a tax deduction. Make sure you get a receipt!

Other tax deductions may be available to you depending on your personal situation. If ever you are in any doubt over what you might be able to claim, you should seek professional advice.

Some tax offsets

A tax offset, or rebate, is not the same thing as a tax deduction—it's much better! Whereas deductions are subtracted from your income in order to work out how much should be taxed, an offset or rebate is deducted directly from your tax payable. Hence it's a much bigger benefit.

Let's look at an example.

Example 11.1: comparing deductions and offsets

Ben earned $65000 in the last tax year. In column A of table 11.3 you can see that he had deductions of $1000. In column B he had no deductions, but did have a tax offset of $1000. Have a look at the table to see how the maths would work.

Table 11.3: example of a tax offset, or rebate

	Column A: tax deduction	Column B: tax offset
Ben's income	$65000	$65000
Less tax deduction	$1000	–
Taxable income	$64000	$65000
Tax payable	$12750	$13050
Plus Medicare levy	$960	$975
Less tax offset	–	$1000
Total tax payable	$13710	$13025

So, tax offsets — because they reduce the amount of tax you have to pay dollar for dollar — are a great benefit!

Common offsets are:

- *Medical expenses*. Have you had any dental work done this year? Laser eye surgery? IVF? If your family has had an expensive time healthwise during the financial year, you may be eligible to claim a medical expenses tax offset. For the 2011–12 financial year it's 20 per cent (that is, 20 cents in the dollar) of your family's net (out-of-pocket) medical expenses over $2000.

- *The education tax refund (for children).* This is also an offset and it enables eligible parents to claim half of most education expenses up to a maximum tax refund of $397 for each primary school child and up to $794 for each secondary school child. Items such as uniforms, home computers and laptops, related computer equipment or repairs, home internet connection and school textbooks can all be claimed. You can check your eligibility and what's available at <www.educationtaxrefund.gov.au>.

- *The private health insurance rebate.* Now, most people claim this offset automatically as a reduction in health insurance premiums. As such you may not even be aware of it. But basically, the government rebates to you a percentage of your private health insurance premium costs. For most people this is a 30 per cent rebate, but it does vary.

- *Childcare tax rebate.* Likewise, with the childcare rebate, many people claim this automatically as reduced fees, or they nominate to receive it periodically from the Family Assistance Office. This is the benefit where the government rebates to eligible parents up to 50 per cent of out-of-pocket childcare expenses, up to a maximum threshold.

There are also additional benefits for making superannuation contributions for seniors and low-income earners. Check out the information that's available on the government's website <www.ato.gov.au>.

The government's decision to raise the tax-free threshold to $18 200 should free up to 1 million people from having to lodge a tax return from 2012–13. Yay!

Step 3: practise good tax habits

All right, so we've had a general overview of the system and a brief glance at some of the most common deductions and offsets. Now, if you're still awake, let's put some good tax habits in place! Nothing too onerous—just a few simple things to help reduce your end-of-financial-year headache.

Keep your receipts

Have a central place where you keep all your receipts. There's nothing worse at the end of the financial year when you have an appointment coming up with your tax agent than not being able to find half the paperwork you need. It doesn't matter if it's a shoebox, a manila folder or something more sophisticated—keep the receipts somewhere that's easily accessible and get in the habit *every day* of throwing any paperwork that could possibly affect your tax there. Whether it's a parking ticket, a stationery receipt, a postage receipt ... throw it in each day, then at the end of the year just sort through it. Easy!

Always ask for a receipt

This leads on from my previous point: remember to ask for a receipt! Whether it's a few dollars handed over to a doorknock appeal, or a trade journal—get a receipt! In order to claim something as a tax deduction you will generally need written proof of payment. So, if a receipt isn't automatically given to you, speak up and ask for one.

Pay your bills

I know it sounds obvious, but we're all busy and it's easy to overlook some of those window-faced envelopes. For an expense to be included in your tax return this year though, it needs to be paid by 30 June. So, if it's going to be a tax deduction for you, pay the bill sooner rather than later so you don't miss the deadline. The difference between paying an expense on 30 June or 1 July is an extra 12-month wait to get the benefit of the deduction!

Understand your marginal tax rate

Your marginal tax rate is the top rate at which you pay tax on your income (remember we talked about this in step 1?). The higher your marginal tax rate, the higher the deduction you receive for expenses, so if your family has a tax-deductible expense that could be paid by either partner (for example, donations), it makes sense to pay this in the name of the partner with the higher marginal tax rate. Let's look at an example.

Example 11.2: marginal tax rates

Table 11.4 shows how the marginal tax rate can affect the refund on a donation.

Table 11.4: refund on a donation at two different marginal tax rates

	Tyrone: marginal tax rate of 37%	Maya: marginal tax rate of 15%
Tax deduction: donation	$1000	$1000
Refund @ marginal tax rate	$370	$150

So, because Tyrone's marginal tax rate is higher, he receives a higher proportion of the donation back into his pocket from his refund.

Seek advice

Tax is a very complex area and quite often you simply don't know what you don't know. Personally, I'd never do my own tax—my accountant does a great job! But whether or not you decide to pay for advice, ensure you do plenty of research on the government's tax website, <www.ato.gov. au>. If you can't afford the cost of an accountant or tax agent, check whether you may be eligible for the ATO's 'Tax Help'. Give them a call on 13 28 61. Tax Help is available from July to October each year to assist low-income earners including seniors, students, people from non–English speaking backgrounds and indigenous Australians.

Research by Bankwest ('Taxing Times' survey, May 2011) found that the average tax refund expected across the country was $2317.

Step 4: other tips and traps

Doing the tasks outlined in step 3 is the most important part of this week. Being organised with your paperwork and prompt with your bill paying are the behaviours that will save you money. But it's worth also mentioning just a few tax-related tips and traps for unwary players.

Keep the Family Assistance Office updated

When it comes to all those family benefits that — if you are a parent — you will be well aware of, your eligibility is partly based on your income. So it's always safer to overestimate your income rather than underestimate it. Otherwise you can end up with a nasty debt at the end of the financial year. So if, when you put your tax paperwork together, you realise that your earnings have changed, make sure you give the Family Assistance Office a call on 13 61 50.

Keep your records for five years

You don't have to send all the paperwork relating to your income and tax deductions to the ATO when you submit your tax return — they'll take your word for it. But they also might decide to audit you, and can request five years' worth of paperwork. So file it away carefully and keep it somewhere safe!

A quick tax deduction

If you're looking for a quick tax deduction hit this year (and you have the cash flow), you can pre-pay up to 12 months' worth of investment or work-related expenses.

In the 2010–11 federal budget it was announced that from 2012–13 the government will provide taxpayers with the choice of a $500 standard deduction to replace deductions for their work-related expenses and cost of managing tax affairs. This will increase to $1000 from 2013–14.

This will enable taxpayers to spend less time and effort preparing their tax return and more time with their family. When fully implemented, 6.4 million Australians will find it easier to choose just the standard deduction and will see their tax drop by an average of $192.

Don't fall for 'tax-effective' scams!

Everyone loves saving tax — but not if it's at the expense of your wealth! No matter how much legislation is put in place, there will always be loopholes for scammers to exploit. The general rule is that tax benefits should always be incidental to any investment you make. So, always, *always* ignore the promised tax benefits and assess an underlying investment on its merits. The Australian Competition and Consumer Commission runs an excellent website, SCAMwatch <www.scamwatch.gov.au>. It's well worth checking out!

Week 12

Spending smart

We have been through so much financial stuff over the course of this book! If you have dutifully read through and completed each week before going on to the next one, you should be feeling pretty pleased with yourself by now!

You've organised a budget, you've collected all your superannuation, you've put plans in place to keep debt under control and you've reviewed just about every type of insurance cover under the sun. You've started organising your estate planning and assessed your mortgage. You've even donned a frilly apron and bustled around the house to implement cost-saving measures such as reducing water usage, conserving electricity and no longer feeding the family dog (just kidding). In short though, you have basically covered the range of day-to-day money issues from A to Z.

You rock! Financially, that is.

So, this final week—these last few money-savvy spending tips—will be a breeze. An absolute breeze. It's really just looking at a few potential traps that drain money from your bank account without adding anything to your lifestyle. By now, given your newly acquired (or recently enhanced) money skills, you can probably guess what they are already. Just to confirm though, we're going to discuss the following steps this week:

1   being fee free

2   using a credit card with rewards points—yes or no?

3   changing payment frequency

4   shopping online

5   thinking about whether you should do extra study.

It will be a piece of cake. So let's get started!

Step 1: be fee free

What's the monthly fee on your savings account? On your transaction account? How about on your mortgage? Unless you have already actively changed your bank accounts to fee-free versions, chances are you'll be paying some monthly transaction or account-keeping fees. All those sneaky charges can really add up! Transaction fees can work out to be more than monthly fees.

Former US vice president Dan Quayle reckoned that bank failures 'are caused by depositors who don't deposit enough money to cover losses due to mismanagement'. We can only hope that he said it in jest, but it nevertheless taps into a fairly widely held 'all-banks-are-bastards' style of view. According to CHOICE's 2010 'Bank Satisfaction' survey, the 'big four' banks fail to keep a whopping 38 per cent of their client base happy.

At the end of the day though, it's up to you to create your own happiness. Banks and other financial institutions are simply that: they're companies that have a duty to make a profit for their shareholders. Charging you fees is part of that whole profit-making exercise. It's not an exercise that you're forced to participate in though, so follow these easy steps.

Abolish regular fees

Here's how you can abolish some of those regular fees:

- *Add up how many accounts you have.* You probably have a transaction account, maybe a cheque account and a savings account. A term deposit? Maybe a bonus saver account, or a cash management account. Talk about (potential) overload! Do you have multiple transaction accounts? Do you really need them?

- *Work out which accounts attract fees.* Generally your transaction account will have either a set monthly account fee or will charge for each individual transaction over a certain limit. Your savings accounts may also have regular fees. Not to mention the one-off foreign ATM fees, late payment fees and overdrawn fees!

- *Jump online and find some fee-free accounts.* Try CANSTAR <www.canstar.com.au>, Mozo <www.mozo.com.au>, InfoChoice <www.infochoice.com.au>, RateCity <www.ratecity.com.au> or CHOICE <www.choice.com.au/betterbanking>.

- *Phone your current provider and ask them to waive the fees/charges on your account.* Before you go to the trouble of opening a new bank account, phone your existing provider and ask what they can do for you. They may just oblige by abolishing the regular fee or transferring your money to an account that better suits your needs.

'Some people are hyper-vigilant about petrol prices but oblivious about paying $2 when withdrawing money out of an ATM ...'

The Australia Institute, 2010

Abolish ad hoc fees

The main ad hoc fees you're likely to incur are overdrawn fees (where you have spent more money than you currently have in your account), foreign ATM fees (the cost imposed on you when you withdraw cash from an ATM that doesn't belong to your bank) and late payment fees (mainly applicable to loans). Some tips to minimise these types of fees include:

- *Check your bank statements regularly.* Obvious, but many of us just don't do it. Internet banking can be a great help in this regard as you can log on and check your transaction history as often as you want. Regular checks can help highlight any sneaky costs that you weren't aware of, and can help you modify your behaviour to avoid them.

- *Avoid foreign ATMs.* The fees to withdraw money from a foreign ATM can be as high as $4 a pop. Do that once or twice a week and it soon adds up! Withdraw cash from your bank's ATMs or as a cash withdrawal on an EFTPOS transaction instead.

- *Do you need branch access?* Fees on bank accounts that include branch access tend to be higher—after all, there are more staff to pay. Sometimes that face-to-face service may be important to you, but for some accounts it's probably not needed.

- *Monitor your bank account balance.* Another benefit of online banking is that it enables you to check accounts each day to ensure you have enough money in your bank account to cover all the outgoings.

- *Set up an automatic debit to pay your loans.* An automatic debit can help avoid late payment fees on your credit cards and other loans. Of course, you will need to make sure you have enough money in your bank account to cover it …! You could investigate getting a small personal overdraft as a standard feature of a product, just to avoid overdraws—particularly on your billing account— as a safeguard that you will be able to pay your bills.

What type of transactor are you?

With hundreds of accounts offered by banks, building societies and credit unions, where do you start when looking for a transaction account that suits your needs? Here are five key tips to help you.

Choosing a transaction account

Are you someone who likes to have lots of cash on them or do you avoid cash at all costs and rely on EFTPOS? Knowing what your behaviour is like and what access you need to your accounts can make your decision much easier. If you need an ATM near your work and home then looking at which ATMs are around these areas can shorten your list. Largely because of ATMs, branch access is becoming far less important to most customers. However, if you do need to visit a branch regularly or would like one handy just in case, keep that in mind when compiling your shortlist.

Compare the costs

Look at the fees and charges associated with each transaction account. Look at them again based on your current habits. After all, it is futile to pay for features you never use. Some transaction accounts will waive fees if you make a regular monthly deposit, such as your salary. Others require you to keep a minimum balance. Only you will know the kind of account that will benefit the way you bank.

What type of transactor are you? (*cont'd*)

Opting for online

Not all online banking is created equal. It is an ever-changing environment and some online banking experiences are superior to others. Some of the things to look at are security, account aggregation and reporting. This all depends on the institution, and a trip into a branch for an online demonstration can be useful. Most banks offer a demonstration site for you to check out their online functionality.

Would you like fries with that?

The financial institution you are considering may have other accounts that would suit you and offer some sort of loyalty rewards to entice you to have other accounts with them. No longer are loyalty programs offered just for home loan packages, so check out what is available. You may be surprised.

What are your plans?

Are your circumstances going to change in the near future? Transaction accounts are a good way to establish a relationship with an institution. If you are looking at taking out a home loan, car loan or maybe looking at moving address it would pay to think 'will my institution be able to support my changing needs and does that matter to me?' By investigating your options for a deposit account that works best, don't discount your current bank as you may find it has the style of account you have been looking for.

Source: CANSTAR <www.canstar.com.au>.

Ask for a better rate! Many banks have promotional rates that they offer to new customers and often those rates expire after a few months. Call your bank and ask for a better rate. A two-minute phone call could work wonders.

Step 2: rewards points — yes or no?

Mmmmm...free flights and accommodation. Movie tickets, cases of wine, shopping vouchers, in-store discounts...there are so many wonderful rewards to be earned, all as a thank-you gift for the mere act of shopping. Could anything be better?

Well, not to be a scrooge but plenty of things could be better as — to quote a cliché — there rarely is such a thing as a free lunch. You can be almost certain that, in some way, shape or form, you are paying for those 'free' rewards!

And are you suited to a rewards card in the first place?

Rewards program — yes or no?

Working out which is the best credit card–based rewards program for you is not as straightforward as you may think. Used correctly, rewards can be worthwhile. After all, chances are you were going to spend that money anyway, so why not get something back for it? On the flipside, a rewards card used wrongly can see you deeper in debt.

To avoid this, there are certain golden rules to follow.

Pay the card off

First, be realistic about whether you pay your card off in full each month or not. As the interest rates on these cards may be higher than that on other credit cards, it's best to pay them off quickly. Otherwise you run the risk of the cost of the card (interest rate plus annual fee) outweighing any rewards benefit you may get. If you can't pay your card off religiously, forget rewards and opt for a low-cost card instead.

Are the rewards offered suitable?

Consider whether the frequent flyer rewards suit your travel needs. For example, if the card offers you a quick way to earn points for flights around Australia but you don't travel domestically very often, ask yourself whether this is a reward you are likely to use. Flights are only one aspect of rewards. You may prefer shopping vouchers, merchandise, travel or cashback.

Rewards program — yes or no? (cont'd)

Examine the fine print

Check the rules first. Before accruing points on a scheme that's hard to redeem points from, be aware of things such as the life span of the points and any rules and restrictions about upgrading on flights.

Pick a card that matches your spend

Choose a rewards program that suits the amount of money you spend on the card every year and is likely, therefore, to give you the best return.

Maximise extra benefits

If you have a Gold or Platinum card and you are earning enough rewards to outweigh your annual fee, benefits such as travel insurance or concierge services effectively come free of charge. Sacrifice some time to read the product disclosure statement in detail so that you know exactly what is available and how you can make use of it to add to the value you get from being with that rewards program.

Source: CANSTAR <www.canstar.com.au>.

According to credit and charge card statistics from the Reserve Bank of Australia, the average amount spent on a credit card each year is about $16000. Plus, the average-sized ongoing debt on that credit card is $3000. So if you are Mr/Ms Average … does having a rewards program stack up? Have a look at table 12.1 to see how the maths could work out.

Table 12.1: average scenario

Card type	Owing	Interest rate and fees	Annual spend	Points value	Interest cost and fees	Total cost of card
Basic 'no frills'	$3000	11% + $30 annual fee	$16000	$0	$311 + $30 = $341	$341
Rewards	$3000	19% + $70 annual fee	$16000	$160	$558 + $70 = $628	$468

Source: Credit card calculator <www.moneysmart.gov.au>.

So in this 'average' scenario, it's potentially costing you an extra $150 or so each year in costs above and beyond the rewards. Not much of a bargain! The main reason for this is that the interest rates on rewards cards tend to be significantly higher than those on a basic, no-frills card. Also, rewards cards tend to have an annual fee (I've chosen a middle-of-the-road fee for the example). The combination of these two extra costs can outweigh any 'rewards' benefits that you manage to accumulate.

Of course, the situation would be different if you spent, say, $60 000 on your credit card each year. In that case the figures would be as shown in table 12.2.

Table 12.2: comparison of credit cards when spending $60 000 per annum

Card type	Owing	Interest rate and fees	Annual spend	Points value	Interest cost and fees	Total cost of card
Basic 'no frills'	$3000	11% + $30 annual fee	$60 000	$0	$311 + $30 = $341	$341
Rewards	$3000	19% + $70 annual fee	$60 000	$600	$558 + $70 = $628	$28

Source: Credit card calculator <www.moneysmart.gov.au>.

In this situation you would be over $300 in front by using a rewards card. And of course if you religiously pay the balance owing from your card each month (as hopefully you eventually will, after having worked your way through week 6), interest repayments are taken out of the equation. This makes it a much easier process to work out whether the rewards stack up. In fact, as you can see from table 12.3 (overleaf), even under the Mr/Ms Average spending scenario you can benefit from having a rewards card.

Table 12.3: $16000 per annum spend, with no outstanding balance

Card type	Owing	Interest rate and fees	Annual spend	Points value	Interest cost and fees	Total cost of card
Basic 'no frills'	$0	11% + $30 annual fee	$16000	$0	$30	$30
Rewards	$0	19% + $70 annual fee	$16000	$160	$70	$90 net gain!

Source: Credit card calculator <www.moneysmart.gov.au>.

However, there are a few absolute golden rules when it comes to using rewards credit cards—and any other form of loyalty card, for that matter. You need to ask yourself some questions.

Is it really a bargain?

Yes, we all like to occasionally tell our respective partners how much we 'saved' by buying that fantastic TV/couch/ bike/pair of shoes while they were on special. But we all know the truth—it's only a bargain if you needed it and would have bought it in the first place. The same is true for your rewards card—if you're buying something simply to boost your rewards points then it's *not* a bargain!

Is it really worthwhile?

It's only worthwhile if you can't get a better deal. Many stores offer a discount when you buy something with cash. That discount can range from 2 per cent to 10 per cent. Given that most rewards cards offer a spend-to-rewards ratio of just 1 per cent, you need to be sensible—it does *not* make sense to use your card if you could get a better deal by paying via another method.

Is there a surcharge?

Ensure you won't incur a surcharge. Not only do some businesses give you a discount for cash—they can also charge an additional fee for credit! Chances are, this surcharge would outweigh the rewards points benefits.

Would you buy it there regardless?

It's only worthwhile if you would have bought it from that location anyway. This pertains more to loyalty cards than to rewards points; nevertheless, it's an interesting exercise in psychology. Whether it's flybuys, a clothing retailer loyalty card or some other form of rewards program, it's easy to become focused on accumulating points rather than genuinely getting a good deal.

Now, the object of this isn't to dissuade you from having and using a rewards points credit card, but just to ensure that—if you do have one—it's a money-savvy choice.

Top tips for finding the best card rewards

- *Credit card rewards schemes are not free.* The best rewards card for you may have an annual fee attached and sometimes an additional fee to cover the rewards program. You need to spend more than a certain amount, which ranges from $12 000 to upwards of $30 000, just to cover the fee. If you're not sure whether you'll spend enough, crunch the numbers. Check previous credit card monthly statements to get an idea of how much you would spend on the card per year.
- *Consider what types of rewards are most valuable for you.* This will help you determine the best rewards program. Plenty of people are happy to redeem their rewards for merchandise. Others prefer to collect air miles, get vouchers for leading retailers, or even make donations to charity. If none of these work for you, consider a card that pays a percentage of your spending back as cash.
- *Do the maths.* Find out exactly how many points you're getting for each dollar you spend and what they translate to in spending power. Rewards points vary from about fifty cents per every $100 spent up to $1.50

Top tips for finding the best card rewards (*cont'd*)

worth of rewards for every $100 spent. Some products tier their rewards so the more you spend, the higher the return.

* *Check the fine print on the rewards card you believe could be the best for you.* For example, your credit card provider can simply drop the one reward that you've always used the card for, such as vouchers for a certain retailer, or change the earn rate. Some points expire over a certain time period, others don't.

Source: CANSTAR <www.canstar.com.au>.

Step 3: payment frequency

Compared with the whole rewards card thing, changing your payment frequency is quick and easy—and what a change it can make! You could be surprised at how much money you can potentially save by changing the payment frequency of your bills. This is the ultimate 'money for nothing' style of saving!

It works because some companies offer a discount for annual payments and because interest on some loans is calculated daily.

Discount for annual payments

This is quite simple: some companies offer a discount for bills that are paid annually. Well, actually, they impose a penalty for bills that are paid monthly, but I'm putting a positive spin on it! Examples of bills that might be cheaper to pay yearly include:

* car/home insurance
* personal insurance
* newspaper and magazine subscriptions
* gym/club memberships.

Table 12.4 gives you a couple of examples.

Table 12.4: discounts for paying premiums annually

Type of expense	Annual cost	Monthly cost	Monthly cost × 12	Additional premium
Home and contents insurance	$1336.77	$128.10	$1537.20	15% extra to pay monthly
Gym membership	$880.00	$95	$1144.00	30% extra to pay monthly

In both instances, it's a significant amount of extra money to pay simply for the convenience of having a shorter time frame. So, go through some of your household bills and check to see whether the cost would reduce if you changed the payment frequency. Seriously, half an hour of paperwork and a few quick phone calls could save you several hundred dollars!

Increase in payment frequency

You can also potentially save a bit of money by *increasing* the payment frequency on some costs — most specifically, your loans!

Remember back in week 7 we discussed your mortgage and the numerous ways to save money on it? Well, one other (albeit modest) way to save a few dollars on your mortgage is to simply change your repayment frequency from monthly to fortnightly. Even without increasing your total annual repayment, you will still save a small amount of money in terms of reduced interest repayments due to the fact that interest is calculated daily.

Look at the example in table 12.5 (overleaf). (Remember our 'original' scenario in week 7.)

Table 12.5: mortgage paid monthly

Loan	$350 000
Term of loan	25 years
Interest rate	8.50%
Monthly repayment	**$2 819 (total annual repayment $33 828)**
Total repayment	**$844 970**
Total amount of interest paid	**$494 970**

So, your alternative here is to keep your annual mortgage repayment the same, but to simply increase the payment frequency. This is shown in table 12.6.

Table 12.6: mortgage paid fortnightly

Loan	$350 000
Term of loan	25 years
Interest rate	8.50%
Fortnightly repayment	**$1 301 (total annual repayment $33 828)**
Total repayment	**$843 489**
Total amount of interest paid	**$493 489**
Saving	**$1 481**

Okay, so it's not very much money—certainly not in comparison to the potential savings you could make by reducing the payment frequency of your other bills—but every bit helps and a two-minute phone call to your bank would probably make it happen.

Step 4: shopping online

Retail is big business—about $242 billion of business per annum. In fact, notwithstanding the mining boom, the retail industry is one of Australia's largest employers. The way we shop has been changing with the rise of technology.

Consumers have been saving significant amounts of money over the past few years by shopping online — chances are you're already on the bandwagon! So, as we have already discussed surfing the net for your insurances, credit cards, loans and superannuation — all your financial products, in other words — in this section I'm going to talk about all those other retail necessities. You know: shoes, clothes, electronics...

Let's look at some stats. According to the Australian Bureau of Statistics, nearly two-thirds of internet users buy stuff online, a figure that rises to more than 80 per cent of 25 to 34-year-olds. Travel, concert and movie tickets, household goods, electrical items, books, clothes and shoes. We love buying them all! PayPal has around 3.5 million active account holders in Australia (a small number compared with their global market share of 100 million active users); eBay has more than 3 million active users. Both companies have double-digit growth. And online sales are still only about 6 per cent of total transactions! The future is looking bright!

In fact, online shopping has been such a rapidly rising force in the retail marketplace over the past decade that we have even had a public enquiry into the implications of globalisation on the Australian retail sector. In their report 'Economic Structure and Performance of the Australian Retail Industry', the Productivity Commission commented that despite our enthusiastic take-up of online shopping, Australia still lags behind a number of comparable countries in terms of volume. The Productivity Commission expects online shopping sales figures to keep growing — something they describe as good for consumers, but challenging for the retail industry. There are some pretty compelling reasons to shop online, including:

- *It's convenient!* No travel time, no parking hassles, no crowds, no getting to a store and finding that they don't have what you want. Online shopping is a quick, convenient, 24-hours-a-day activity. Why wouldn't you use it?

- *It's easy to compare prices.* Unlike trudging from store to store or spending an hour or two phoning around, you can use the internet to compare the prices of a specific item within a few minutes. So easy!

- *It's cost-effective.* A whole host of expenses are cheaper for online retailers. There are generally fewer wages and lower rent, and with our currently healthy Australian dollar we have currency power as well! All these variables often help to make it more cost-effective to buy online from both Australian-based and international online stores.

- *There's a huge range of products.* The world is your oyster? Maybe or maybe not, but the world is fast becoming your shopping mall!

So, when it comes to online retailers, who are the best? According to the Australian Consumers Association, which runs an annual 'People's CHOICE Award' through its consumer website, the most popular online retailers for 2010 were as shown in table 12.7.

'Finding something on sale is the emotional equivalent of a small lotto win for many shoppers ...'

The Australia Institute, 2011

Online shopping isn't 100 per cent retail nirvana though. A November 2010 report created by the Australian Communications and Media Authority (ACMA) titled 'Australia in the Digital Economy — Consumer Engagement in e-commerce' found evidence of a perceived risk in transacting online, with one-quarter of survey respondents indicating a lack of trust in the internet.

Table 12.7: most popular online retailers, 2010

Rank	Retailer	Votes
1	eBay	2442
2	Apple	542
3	Amazon	536
4	Deals Direct	333
5	Ticketek	296
6	Ezibuy	270
7	Catch of the Day	225
8	The Book Depository	195
9	GETPRICE	182
10	StrawberryNET	174

Source: <www.choice.com.au/choiceawards>.

According to the CHOICE survey, the most popular online shopping site by far was eBay with 47 per cent of the vote. It's probably not surprising given that there are over 50 000 product categories and over 2 million people logging on to <www.ebay.com.au> each day. It's also perhaps testament to the fact that being first into the market reaps huge benefits. While there are other online auction sites in Australia, none have anywhere near the popularity of eBay. Apple and Amazon — also both household names — received 10 per cent of the vote each. And Ticketek, our largest sports and entertainment ticketing company, ranked fifth on the list. Strawberrynet just scraped in to the top 10 with a modest 3 per cent of the vote.

An interesting inclusion on the list was Catch of the Day — a group buying website that acts as a clearing house for well-known brands. Group buying sites are still in their infancy in Australia and the jury is still out as to whether they will be a long-term success. But there may well be more of them on the list in years to come.

It does make sense to exercise some caution and common sense when transacting. Here are some safety tips:

- *Buy from well-known and reputable sites.* Some larger sites and payment systems have buyer protection insurance.

- *Use a secure payment system.* Paypal is a good example.

- *Make sure you know what you're buying.* Read the online product description carefully to ensure you are buying the item you want.

- *Keep copies of purchase and payment confirmations.* Just as you should keep your physical shopping dockets (at least for a while), you should safely file your online shopping confirmations as well.

- *Avoid letting anyone know your personal password.* We have all, I'm sure, received those 'security' emails purporting to be from financial institutions; a legitimate business will never ask for your password over the phone or via email.

- *Create a difficult-to-guess password.* Don't use the same password for multiple websites.

- *Avoid clicking on links in emails that you are unsure about.* It is always safer to manually type the website address of a business directly into your computer.

- *Have up-to-date anti-virus software on your computer.*

- *Check out the government's SCAMwatch website.* SCAMwatch is run by the Australian Competition and Consumer Commission (ACCC). It provides some excellent information to consumers about how to recognise, avoid and report scams. You can check them out and download their 'Little Black Book of Scams' at <www.scamwatch.gov.au>.

Online shopping can be fantastic fun and can save you heaps. As with any form of shopping though, a bit of common sense goes a long way!

Step 5: extra study

It might seem a bit counter-intuitive in a book about saving money, but despite the upfront cost of tertiary study, the economic reality is that university graduates earn, on average, significantly more than non-graduates over their working life.

In fact according to an AMP and NATSEM report on the costs of tertiary education in Australia ('What Price the Clever Country?') a university graduate has the potential to earn an extra $1.5 million, compared with those whose highest qualification is Year 12. And with average university fees for a Bachelor degree totalling $20 579, that's a damn fine return on investment!

Sure, there could be a few years of financial pain while you study (the average uni student has only about one-third the amount of income of a similarly aged full-time worker) but the long-term gains are potentially worth it. Of course, your career is much more than a financial connect-the-dots exercise. You also need genuine interest, passion and aptitude. Nevertheless, it's worth thinking about.

After all, you're already a savings expert now; you'll surely need *something* else to occupy your time!

Appendix A

Balance sheet

Complete this balance sheet for your current situation. It should list everything you own on the left-hand side and everything you owe on the right.

Assets	$ value	Liabilities	$ value
House		Mortgage 1	
Contents		Mortgage 2	
Transaction accounts		Overdraft	
Other accounts		Credit cards	
Term deposits		Store cards	
Managed funds*		Car loan	
Shares		Other personal loans	
Investment property		Investment loan 1	
Other investments		Investment loan 2	
Car		Tax liability	
Car		Other:	
Boat/caravan/other			
Share of business			
Share of family trust			
Other:			
Total		**Total**	
Total Assets $_____ less		**Total Liabilities $_____ =**	
		Net Worth $_____	

* Do not include funds held within superannuation.

Appendix B

Annual budget

Income	$ per month	Annual amount
Your take-home pay		
Your partner's take-home pay		
Bonuses/Overtime		
Income from savings and investments		
Centrelink benefits		
Family benefit payments		
Child support received		
Other:		
Financial commitments		
Rent/Mortgage		
Car loan repayments		
Other loan repayments		
Credit-card interest		
Voluntary super payments		
Savings		
Child-support payments		
Donations/Charity		
Pocket money		
Other:		

Home	$ per month	Annual amount
Council rates		
Body corporate fees		
Home and contents insurance		
Home maintenance and repairs		
New furniture/appliances		
Other:		
Utilities		
Electricity		
Gas		
Water		
Internet		
Pay TV		
Home phone		
Mobile phone(s)		
Other:		
Education		
School fees		
Uni/TAFE		
Childcare/Preschool		
School uniforms		
Sport/Music/Dance etc.		
Excursions		
Other:		
Health		
Private health insurance		
Life insurance		
Doctors		

Dentists		
Medicines/Pharmacy		
Eye care/Glasses		
Vet		
Other:		

Shopping/Transport		
Supermarket		
Fruit/Vegetables		
Baby products		
Clothing/Shoes		
Cosmetics/Toiletries		
Hairdresser		
Gifts/Other		
Other food/Groceries:		
Car insurance		
Car maintenance		
Registration/Licence		
Petrol		
Road tolls/Parking		
Trains/Buses/Ferries		
Other:		

Entertainment		
Holidays		
Bars/Clubs		
Other alcohol		
Gym/Sporting membership		
Cigarettes		

Entertainment (*cont'd*)	$ per month	Annual amount
Movies/Music		
Hobbies		
Newspaper/Magazines		
Celebrations		
Other:		
Eating out		
Restaurants		
Takeaway/Snacks		
Bought lunches		
Coffee/Tea		
Other:		
TOTAL SUMMARY: INCOME – EXPENSES =		

Appendix C

Health insurance — what do I need?

With so many different health insurance policies to choose from, writing down a few of the things that are important to you can help to narrow your search and save you some valuable time.

How much hospital cover do I need?	
How much excess can I afford to pay?	
Can I afford a co-payment?	
Can I afford to pay a gap fee? How much?	
Which hospitals do I need to be covered for?	
Do I need extras? Which ones?	

Appendix D

Asset classes

While there are hundreds of different types of investment, they all relate back to four main asset classes.

Cash

The simplest example of a cash investment is a bank account on which you earn interest. In this situation, you are lending money to an institution in return for interest payments. Generally, a cash investment has a short investment timetable and provides a stable, low-risk income.

Bonds

When you invest in bonds, you are lending to either the government or a corporation, usually for a set period of time at a set interest rate. Often, the higher the interest rate, the higher the potential risk.

Bonds vary from very safe to quite risky and most bonds do have a credit rating. The value of a bond will rise or fall depending on the current interest rate. The Reserve Bank of Australia has some useful information on its website <www.rba.gov.au> on buying and selling bonds.

Property

We all know what property is—but there are so many different types: residential, retail, commercial and industrial, just to name a few of the more common ones.

You can invest in property in two ways:

- directly—where you buy a specific piece of real estate in your own name

- indirectly—where you invest in a managed fund that uses pooled investor funds to buy real estate.

Return from property is in two parts: capital growth (although note that property can fall in price as well as rise) and rental income.

Shares

A share represents part ownership of a company. When you buy a share, you are buying a small slice of ownership. Shares can be bought directly—generally via the stock exchange—or indirectly through a managed fund. Similarly to property, returns from shares usually include capital growth and income through dividends.

Appendix E

Key home loan facts

In January 2012 the National Consumer Credit Protection Amendment introduced compulsory, one-page key fact sheets for new home loan customers. This has made it easier to compare your mortgage with other products on the market.

The fact sheets give consumers a basic overview of the interest rate, the 'all-in' rate (rate including other fees), the total cost of the mortgage over time, the features included and an indication of what would happen to your repayments if rates increased.

Overleaf is a sample of a key home loan facts sheet.

KEY FACTS ABOUT THIS HOME LOAN	
Date produced: 1 December 2011	[lender logo] Australian credit licence number: [lender's ACL number] [1]
THIS IS NOT AN OFFER OF CREDIT. This Key Facts Sheet is provided to help you compare this home loan with the home loans of other lenders.	
What you have told us	
Loan amount: $300 000	**[loan amount]**
Term of the home loan:	**[loan term]**
Interest type:	**[fixed or variable]** [2]
Lender and product name:	**[lender and product name]**
HOW DOES THIS HOME LOAN COMPARE?	
Description of this home loan	
Repayment method	Principal and interest [3]
Repayment frequency	Monthly (other repayment options are available) [4]
Interest rate	[5] **[variable interest rate]** per annum **[fixed interest rate]** per annum fixed for **[number]** years, then a variable rate currently **[variable interest rate]** per annum **[introductory interest rate]** per annum for **[number]** years, then a variable rate currently [variable interest rate] per annum
Personalised comparison rate: (interest rate including fees)	**[Personalised comparison rate]** per annum [6]

Estimated cost of this home loan	
Total amount to be paid back (including the loan amount and fees)[1]	**[repaid amount]** [7]
This means you will pay back	**[amount] for every $1 borrowed** [8]
Establishment fees	**[establishment fees]** [9]
Ongoing fees	**[monthly fees]** [11] **per month** **[annual fees]** [12] **per year**
[10] Repayment per month (including ongoing fees)	**[monthly repayment]** [13]
[10] Repayment per year (including ongoing fees)	**[yearly repayment]** [14]
[10] Repayment per month for first [number] [15] years (including ongoing fees)	**[monthly repayment]** [13]
[10] Repayment per year for first [number] [15] years (including ongoing fees)	**[yearly repayment]** [14]
[10] Repayment per month after [number] [15] years (including ongoing fees)	**[monthly repayment]** [13]
[10] Repayment per year after [number] [15] years (including ongoing fees)	**[yearly repayment]** [14]

There may be circumstances in which other fees are payable. Fees applicable for the loan you apply for will be shown in the loan contract. You can also obtain a list of fees applicable to this type of loan from our branches [16] or through our website at [lender's website]. Other loan set-up fees, such as valuation fees and lender's mortgage insurance, and Government charges, such as registration fees and stamp duty on property transfer, have not been included. These will be determined after application. Additional fees may be payable if you choose to repay your fixed rate home loan early. [17]

[18] What happens at the end of the fixed rate period?

At the end of the fixed rate period you may be able to fix the rate at a new fixed interest rate for a further period. If a further fixed rate is not entered into, the rate will convert to the applicable variable interest rate. Under the current variable interest rate, if interest rates do not change, your monthly repayment would **[increase/decrease]** by around **[change in repayment]**

[18] What happens if interest rates increase?

This is a variable rate loan. If your interest rate was to increase by 1% per annum, your monthly repayment would increase by around **[change in repayment 2]**[19]. This is a fixed rate loan. Your repayments will not change during the fixed rate period. After the fixed rate period, if the variable interest rate was to increase by 1% per annum, from the current variable interest rate of [variable interest rate], your monthly repayment would increase by around **[change in repayment]**[18].

How can I repay my loan faster?

This loan allows you to make additional repayments to pay off your home loan faster. If you increased your monthly repayments by $200 a month to **[monthly repayment + $200]** you would repay the loan in **[new loan term]**, instead of **[loan term]**, based on the current variable interest rate stated in this Key Facts Sheet.[19] This loan allows you to make additional repayments to pay off your loan faster but such repayments may attract a fee. You should ask your lender about the fee before making additional repayments. [19]

This loan does not allow you to make additional repayments to pay off your home loan faster. [19]

Altering the frequency of repayments may also help repay the loan faster.

How to find the best deal for you

To obtain the best deal for you, it is important to shop around and compare interest rates, fees and features before you apply for a home loan. Choosing the best home loan for you may save you money. For more information about how to get the best deal on your home loan visit the ASIC consumer website at <www.moneysmart.gov.au>.

Notes in model of Key Facts Sheet: A lender that prepares a Key Facts Sheet for a particular consumer must include the following information at the numbers marked in the model:

[1] If the lender is an ACL holder – this is the lender's ACL number. If the lender is not an ACL holder, no ACL number is required. However, the lender must disclose that the credit provider's ACL will be provided in the credit contract. The lender is exempted from the requirement to set out its ACN or ABN in subsection 153(2) of the *Corporations Act 2001* on the Key Facts Sheet.

[2] This must be an interest type in the table in regulation 28LA. If a fixed loan is specified, the term of the fixed rate period must also be indicated.

[3] Under regulation 28LA, the repayments under the home loan must repay principal and interest for the full term of the loan.

[4] The repayment frequency must be based on monthly repayments.

[5] This is the current interest rate applicable to the loan on the date on which the Key Facts Sheet is produced. If discounts to this interest rate apply, the discount and the period in which it will apply must also be disclosed here. Only one of the 4 paragraphs in this box is required. Omit the paragraphs that do not apply to the loan this Key Facts Sheet relates to.

[6] This rate must be calculated in accordance with the formula in subregulation 100 (3) but using the designated amounts provided by the consumer under sections 133AC and 133AD of the Act. This rate includes each fee or charge (if any) payable by the debtor at the time each repayment is made, being a credit fee or charge (other than a government fee, charge or duty) that is ascertainable when the comparison rate is disclosed (whether or not the credit fee or charge is payable if the credit is not provided). The tolerances in subregulations 100 (4), (5) and (6) also apply to this rate.

[7] This is the sum of the principal and all interest and fees certain to be payable over the life of the home loan. The fees include each fee or charge (if any) payable by the debtor at the time each repayment is made, being a credit fee or charge (other than a government fee, charge or duty) that is ascertainable when the comparison rate is disclosed (whether or not the credit fee or charge is payable if the credit is not provided).

[8] This is the total amount to be paid back, divided by the loan amount, expressed as a dollar amount for every dollar borrowed.

[9] These are the fees and charges, paid to the lender on the commencement of the loan, used for the purpose of calculating the Personalised Comparison Rate.

[10] If the home loan is a variable rate loan or a fixed rate loan with a term that expires at the end of the fixed rate period, only the first 2 sections ('Repayment per month (including ongoing fees)' and 'Repayment per year (including ongoing fees)') are required. If the home loan is any other type of standard home loan, the remaining sections are required.

[11] This is any fee paid each month to the lender on a regular and ongoing basis.

[12] This is any fee paid each year to the lender on a regular and ongoing basis. It does not include the monthly ongoing fee in note 11.

[13] This is the sum of amounts payable per month on the home loan and any fees that are charged in that month.

[14] This is the sum of the amounts payable per year on the home loan and any fees that are charged during the year.

[15] This is the length of the fixed rate period for fixed loans, the length of the discount rate period for introductory rate loans, and the length of the period before the discounted rate applies for discounting rate loans.

[16] The reference to the lender's branches in this sentence may be removed if not applicable.

[17] Only include if break fees are payable on the loan.

[18] Omit this section if the interest rate will be fixed for the entire term of the loan.

[19] Only one of these paragraphs is required. Omit the paragraph that does not apply to the loan this Key Facts Sheet relates to.

Assumptions

The tolerances and assumptions under section 180 of the Code apply to the calculation of any amounts in this Key Facts Sheet.

Publication online

If a Key Facts Sheet is published online, links must be provided to the websites mentioned in the Key Facts Sheet.

Adopting the Key Facts Sheet for non-prescribed purposes

A lender may produce a Key Facts Sheet for home loans if Part 3-2A of the Credit Act does not require the lender to provide a Key Facts Sheet. A lender that provides such a Key Facts Sheet must, to a reasonable extent, comply with the requirements for producing the Key Facts Sheet, but must omit any reference to the production of the Key Facts Sheet being an Australian Government requirement.

Note

All legislative instruments and compilations are registered on the Federal Register of Legislative Instruments kept under the Legislative Instruments Act 2003. See http://www.frli.gov.au.

FURTHER INFORMATION ABOUT THIS KEY FACTS SHEET

Which home loan is right for you?

When choosing a home loan, it's important to work out what you want from your loan and how much it will cost you. Given the wide range of loans on offer – with different interest rates, product features and fees – it pays to shop around to find the loan that fits your needs and circumstances. Some loans offer features that may be appropriate for your situation and result in savings over the life of the loan.

Some features you may wish to consider include:

- ability to split your loan between fixed and variable interest rates;

- ability to make extra repayments;

- an offset account;

- a redraw facility; and

- linked credit card and savings accounts.

But compare the costs and benefits of these features before you agree to them. For more information on choosing the right home loan for you, you may also wish to visit the ASIC consumer website at <www.moneysmart.gov.au>.

Where can I find out more about this loan?

If you want more information on the terms used in this document or about this home loan, please contact us [lender's contact details], or visit our website at [lender's contact website].

This Key Facts Sheet is an Australian Government requirement.

The Australian Government requires all lenders selling standard home loans to give you a Key Facts Sheet like this one when you ask for one and provide the necessary information.

Key Facts Sheets contain information presented in the same way to help you compare and select the most appropriate home loan for you. You should request Key Facts Sheets when shopping around for a home loan to help you find the home loan that is right for you.

This Key Facts Sheet is not an offer of credit. The lender is not obliged to provide you with the home loan described in this Key Facts Sheet. You will need to apply for the loan and meet our lending criteria before we can determine whether you are eligible for this loan.

You should also be aware:

- the interest rates and fees and charges are those that apply as at the

- date of production of this Key Facts Sheet.

- the amount required to be paid does not include fees which are

- dependent on events that may not occur (for example, late payment

- fees if you do not make repayments on time).

- the amount of the repayments shown in this Key Facts Sheet will

- change if interest rates, fees and charges change and if a different loan

- type, loan term or loan amount is used.

What is the personalised comparison rate?

The personalised comparison rate helps you understand what the total cost of your home loan might be, taking into account known fees and charges that will apply (other than government fees, charges or duties) by building those costs into the interest rate. It also helps you understand the impact of fixed or introductory rates of interest on the total amount of interest you could pay over the life of the loan.

For more information about home loans visit the ASIC financial tips website: <www.fido.gov.au>.

Websites that compare home loan products include: CHOICE Better Banking <betterbanking.choice.com.au>, CANSTAR <www.canstar.com.au>, InfoChoice <www. infochoice.com.au>, RateCity <www.ratecity.com.au>, and Money Zone or Mozo <www.mozo.com.au>.

Index

Printed and bound by CPI Group (UK) Ltd, Croydon, CR0 4YY